# The Observant Traveller

Association of County Archivists

# The Observant Traveller

**Diaries of Travel in England, Wales and Scotland
in the County Record Offices of
England and Wales**

Edited by Robin Gard

London   Her Majesty's Stationery Office

© Crown Copyright 1989
First published 1989

ISBN 0 11 701208 4

Front cover

George Richardson  (1807–1840)

*The Stage Coach Road,
Northumberland*

Laing Art Gallery
Newcastle upon Tyne

# Contents

# Acknowledgements

The Association of County Archivists gratefully acknowledges the courtesy of the following owners of diaries deposited in county record offices in allowing extracts to be published in this book, and is similarly obliged to owners of the additional illustrative material reproduced with their kind permission:

Mrs Pamela Antrobus   (106)
Bedfordshire County Council   (64, 115)
Revd. J. D. Bickersteth   (17)
Mr Justin Blaythwayt   (81, 109, 110)
The Bodleian Library   (20)
Lt. Col. W. Kemmis Buckley   (66, 68)
Cheshire County Council   (99)
Mrs P. S. S. Clifford   (3)
Clwyd County Council   (29–32, 61, 78, 120)
Sir John Colfox   (131)
Mr T. W. E. Corbett   (129)
The Rt. Hon. the Viscount Cross   (7)
Cumbria County Council   (52–55)
The Rt. Hon. the Viscount Daventry   (116, 117)
The Rt. Hon. the Earl of Denbigh   (27)
Derbyshire Archaeological Society   (43)
Devon County Council   (44–47, 51, 121, 122, 132, 134)
Doncaster Metropolitan Borough Council   (28)
Durham County Council   (13)
East Sussex County Council   (14)
Essex County Council   (84, 85, 89, 93, 111, 127, 128)
Mr E. Lloyd Francis   (10)
Miss Marigold Graham, J. P.   (60, 72)
Margaret, Lady Guise   (50)
Gwynedd County Council   (63)
Mrs J. R. Halford   (40, 91)
Hampshire County Council   (8, 9, 18, 75, 123–126, 137)
The Exors. of Lt. Col. J. C. E. Harding-Rolls, M.C., D.L., J.P. (113, 114)
Mr Simon Heneage   (16)
Mrs P. Henderson   (37)
Hereford and Worcester County Council   (105)

Hertfordshire County Council   (103)
Isle of Wight County Council   (6, 49, 88)
Kent County Council   (7A, 41)
Lancashire County Council   (56, 57)
The Trustees of the Estate of Mr Nella Leicester   (15)
The Trustees of the Lonsdale Estate Trust   (69)
The Exors. of Major F. W. Lowndes-Stone-Norton   (2)
The Rt. Hon. The Lady Lucas   (100, 102)
Miss Susan Mackay   (24)
The National Trust   (48, 67, 77, 119)
Newcastle upon Tyne Central Library   (87A)
Newcastle upon Tyne Laing Art Gallery   (6A)
New Lanark Conservation   (73)
Norfolk County Council   (22, 38)
Northumberland County Council   (1, 42, 71, 87, 108)
Nottinghamshire County Council   (25, 34, 130)
Mr Philip Pendarves   (58, 59, 79, 80, 82, 83, 98)
Major H. R. M. Porter   (12)
Miss S Pugh-Jones   (92, 107)
The Rt. Hon. the Viscount Ridley, T.D.   (5, 35, 62, 104)
Mrs R. Rostas   (74, 76)
Mr R. C. Sayer   (36, 39)
Col. P. F. Shakerley   (21)
Somerset Archaeological and Natural History Society   (33)
Somerset County Council   (101)
Mr Ralph Stepney-Gulston   (65)
Suffolk County Council   (96, 97, 118)
Surrey County Council   (135)
Mr G. E. Peter Thornhill   (23, 70, 94)
Mrs C. E. Townley   (4)
Valentines of Dundee Ltd.   (136)
Miss P. A. C. Wallington   (19, 86)
The Walker Art Gallery   (26)
Lt. Col. H. J. Weld   (112)
Mrs Margaret Williams   (90)
Lt. Col. Sir Watkin Williams-Wynn, Bt., C.B.E.   (11)

# Foreword

The twentieth century has seen an enormous development in the speed with which visual images can be transmitted and created. Unfortunately, many of these are highly transitory and leave but a half-remembered impact on the mind.

Not so the many diary extracts contained in this publication. Lovingly and carefully created by their writers, such diaries are splendid examples of the use of words in describing journeys made, folk encountered and sights experienced. In times when instant-print photography was not dreamt of and picture postcards and souvenirs unknown, the writings of diarists were their only permanent recollection – outside the memory itself – and provide us today with immediate contemporary accounts of life, society and the environment.

Most travel diaries do not relate to the writer's home ground and for this reason a diary about Northumberland may, for example, be amongst the personal papers of, say, a Devon man or woman and located in a Record Office in his or her home County. The Association of County Archivists has long been aware that many County Record Offices contain a great many records relating to other counties and is naturally anxious that such information be as widely published and disseminated as possible.

The book is modelled on *The Common Chronicle* published by the Association to mark its major exhibition of archive treasures from local Record Offices held at the Victoria and Albert Museum in 1983 and at Leicester in 1987. There is undoubtedly an enormous wealth of material in County Record Offices, much of it known about and widely used but also much of which has yet to be tapped, at least in any formal historical way.

The work of County Record Offices is often not widely known, rather unglamorous at times and certainly always in need of enhancement. Nevertheless an enormous amount is achieved, by caring local authorities anxious to prevent the dispersal or loss of their local or archival heritage and by highly public-spirited owners, large numbers of whom place equally large quantities of family and other archives in Record Offices either as gifts or loans. Without this quiet and magnanimous action on the part of depositors, an important part of our local and national background would scarcely be known, let alone available to researchers and the public at large.

My thanks must go to the Officers of the Association who have helped steer the publication along its administrative path, and to the many archivists throughout the country who have taken the trouble to list, examine, select extracts, and obtain permission to publish. Thanks are due also to HMSO for their willing co-operation and funding without which publication would have been impossible. All these are, however, overshadowed by the immense amount of work undertaken by the editor, Robin Gard, former County Archivist of Northumberland. Without his diligence, foresight and perseverance, this book would not be the excellent work it is or may not even have come to fruition. The laurels are his.

Tony Wherry
Chairman, Association of County Archivists
March 1988

# Introduction

For centuries, people who liked to explore the countryside and had the time and money to indulge their interest, having exhausted what their immediate neighbourhood had to offer, journeyed further afield to see what other parts of the country were like. On such travels many noted down their impressions in diaries which were doubtless read later by family and friends for the pleasure of recollection, in much the same way as one would look at holiday photographs today. The books themselves would then remain among the family papers until eventually they found their way with the rest of the family's archives into a county record office.

Most travel diaries contain information mainly about places beyond the boundaries of the county in which the traveller lived, and thus as historical documents they are much more likely to be of interest to historians of the places visited than of the home county. But how, for instance, would an Essex historian get to know that the Somerset Record Office holds the diary of John Walker, an unrepentant Parliamentarian, describing a visit to Colchester in 1672 (*16*, **502**)[1], or a Somerset historian discover that the Clwyd office has Elizabeth Giffard's diaries about life in Bath in 1766 (*29, 30*, **54**)? Many record offices, it is true, have published guides to their records, but these have tended to concentrate on official county records and other familiar classes of documents mainly of internal county interest. Subject guides are rare, which makes the *Guides to Sources for British History*, published by HMSO for the Royal Commission on Historical Manuscripts, and which includes documents in county record offices, a welcome series. Even so, up till now there has been no integrated guide to any class of documents deposited in county record offices. The main object of *The Observant Traveller* is thus to identify every original diary of travel in England, Wales and Scotland deposited in the country's forty-nine county record offices and to indicate by extracts the sort of information they contain.

The record offices have cooperated wholeheartedly in the venture and this guide is the product of a combined operation between the staffs of the offices and myself. Each office was asked to supply a list of deposited

---

[1] *Italic* numbers refer to extracts, **bold** to catalogue entries.

diaries in a common form. Originally, it was hoped to describe each diary in some detail, and even indicate its main subject interest, but when it was found that the number of diaries would run into hundreds it was decided to restrict the description to a note of the counties visited by the traveller. The only exceptions were that towns and other places would be noted when the diary was simply a record of a journey between two named places, and also where the visit was clearly to a single place, such as Bath or Oxford, rather than to the county generally. In some cases, too, only the region or country is identified. The relevant record office will gladly supply further details of any listed diary. Some offices, notably Bedfordshire, Cambridgeshire and Cornwall, already have detailed lists available and Suffolk and West Sussex are among offices which have published summary lists in local publications. The preliminary survey, incidentally, covered diaries of travel abroad and it was found that there were about two such diaries for every one of home travel.

A catalogue of travel diaries identifying simply the names of places visited without any indication of the sort of information they contain would have limited use and interest. Each office was therefore also asked to supply sample extracts from their diaries, and the first part of the book presents a selection of these designed principally to demonstrate the range and quality of the historical evidence they provide. The classification is a personal one, and beyond this selection and the random samples from which they have been chosen lies an almost inexhaustible stock of similar and possibly richer material which no one person could examine and describe adequately. It is hoped that *The Observant Traveller* will at least introduce the reader to a class of historical documents which has hitherto been largely overlooked, and encourage exploration.

The catalogue comprises 608 diaries written by some 360 diarists. The actual number of separate journeys described is probably well over 700, since because of variations in cataloguing, diaries of one traveller relating to separate tours have been listed individually in one county office and collectively in another. The diaries are almost all in book form, and vary in length from over 300 pages to a mere four or five, and in size from folio volumes to very small pocket books. Forty-six of the diaries are also illustrated, a few with inserted engravings but most with sketches drawn by the diarists themselves, some of whom were accomplished artists. The watercolours and sketches of Luttrell Wynne in 1771 (*80*, **70**), the Rev John Swete in 1788 and 1789 (*45*, **111**, *47*, **115**), and Robert Parker in 1804 (*124*, *126*, **263**) are works of merit, while the informal sketches of Frederica Rouse-Boughton in 1860 (*64*, *115*, **25**) and Laura Palmer in 1871 (*75*, *13*, **271**) are delightful. A sketch of Cromer made in 1825 by a Mr Marten (*38*, **396**) in a diary deposited in the Norfolk Record Office was found to match almost exactly a description of the resort in 1821 in a diary of John Thornton (*37*, **446**) in the Northamptonshire office. One diarist, Mary Anne Hibbert (**219–228**), refers almost daily in her diary to sketching but, unfortunately, no sketches were found. The illustrations in the diaries, whether original drawings or contemporary engravings, constitute an important visual record, and are particularly valuable when related directly to the text. Some of the illustrations in the book, however, have been selected from other contemporary sources.

In date, the diaries range from Christopher Lowther's Scottish tour of 1629 (*69*, **91**) to notebooks of Albert Batty (**251**) in the 1970s. Five diaries date from the seventeenth century and there are twenty from 1700 to 1750, 140 from 1750 to 1800, 270 from 1800 to 1850, 130 from 1850 to 1900, and forty in the present century.

Other than titles and life dates, the catalogue gives little indication of the status of the diarists themselves, although since travellers had to have both time and money to travel, it may safely be assumed that they mostly belonged to the leisured upper and middle classes. Clearly identified are thirty-six members of the nobility and gentry and their ladies, and sixteen clergymen, while eighty-four diarists were women. Many went on annual tours or holidays and filled several books with accounts of their wanderings. Twelve diarists left more than ten books each, including John Brown's seventy-nine pocket books from 1889 to 1959 (**144**), R W Shooter's forty volumes, each of some 200 pages, from 1910 to 1966 (**325**), and the twenty-nine volumes of Leslie Todd from 1924 to 1967 (**563**). Of earlier diarists, the Rev John Swete completed twenty-two volumes from 1788 to 1801 (**111–116**), Katherine Plymley fourteen volumes from 1794 to 1814 (**480–493**), and George Eaton twenty-two volumes from 1848 to 1895 (**402–419**).

Extracts from several of the diaries have been published, mostly in the transactions of county antiquarian societies, but only five have been published in full, those of Christopher Lowther, 1629 (**91**), Ralph Thoresby, 1677–1724 (**595**), M de Blainville, 1703 (**210**), William George Maton, 1794 (**110**), and Abigail Gawthern, 1802 (**464**). The diaries of Lowther and Maton are among the 135 or so published diaries listed by G E Fussell in *The Exploration of England: A Select Bibliography of Travel and Topography: 1570–1815* in 1935. This book contains unpublished diaries of two other diarists in Fussell's list: a short diary of George, Lord Lyttelton for 1755 (**52**), and four late eighteenth century journals of Thomas Pennant (**58, 582–584**).

Some of the earliest diaries are little more than notes of journeys, giving merely distances between towns; inns, expenses and similar details. However, in the high period of touring in the late eighteenth and first half of the nineteenth centuries, some tours were evidently extensive. In 1765 George Culley travelled from Northumberland to Leicestershire, toured the Midlands and southern counties, visited London and returned home through most of the eastern counties (*42*, **451**), while Frances Bridger's travels in 1768 and 1772 took her through fifteen counties (**156**). A few diarists noted down the distances travelled and T J Parke, on a tour of 1049 miles in 1813, calculated the distances travelled by different conveyances (*5*, **458**).

The index shows that there are 150 diaries recording visits to Scotland and 100 to Wales. Yorkshire, with 101 visits, was the county most visited, followed by Cumbria, then Cumberland and Westmoreland. Some 78 visits to London are recorded, 66 to Lancashire, including Manchester and Liverpool, and 63 to Devon, while Cornwall, Somerset, Gloucestershire, the Isle of Wight, Oxfordshire, Kent, Derbyshire and Nottinghamshire also attracted many tourists. Bedfordshire, Essex and Suffolk were less popular and the large number of diaries held in these offices suggests that people in these counties were among the keenest travellers.

Parke's list (5, **458**) of the various conveyances employed is exceptional as few diarists seem to say much about methods of travel: the vehicles in which they travelled are more likely to be mentioned when something untoward occurred. Many evidently travelled in their own carriages, hiring horses on the way; others took post chaises, gigs and the other popular horsedrawn vehicles of the day, while others went on horseback or by coach. Travelling before the railway era was slow and tedious, to judge from the experience of the diarist whose post chaise took two and a half hours to complete the ten mile journey (albeit on a stony and gated road) from Yarmouth to Newport in the Isle of Wight in 1776, although his party seem to have diverted themselves agreeably (6, **326**). Inns, lodgings, food and their cost feature regularly, and some diarists took the trouble to jot down itineraries for future reference (3).

The journeys of the earlier travellers were largely confined to the principal routes, and there are many descriptions of the towns where they stayed overnight or longer, noting the buildings, trades, occupations, and general character – for example, the visits to Winchester in 1687 (17, **154**), Norwich in 1757 (21, **67**), and Liverpool in 1764 (25, **463**). Travelling for health and pleasure to take the waters at Bath and other spas became fashionable from the middle of the eighteenth century (29, 30, **54**), and towards the end of the century sea-bathing came into vogue and Weymouth (34, **464**) and Brighton (36, **162**) became popular by royal patronage. At about the same time the more adventurous, guided by more detailed road books and enabled to travel faster and further by better main roads, began to explore the wild and mountainous regions of North Wales, the Lakes and Scotland. A number of diarists travelled with the serious intent of improving their knowledge. Lord Grantham visited the principal manufacturing towns in 1799 noting, among other matters, the processes of silver plating at Sheffield and cotton spinning at Manchester (100, 102, **17**), and George Culley toured half the country in 1765 to observe agricultural methods (**451**). Well over half the diaries were written between 1770 and 1850, the period in which Britain's economy was transformed, and the diaries provide something of a running commentary on the industrial and agrarian revolutions.

The personality of the diarist emerges almost immediately and can be perceived even from the brief extracts, and the style of writing varies from the ponderous to the positively lighthearted. The majority of diarists seem to have been of fairly cheerful disposition, and one can only admire them for their philosophical acceptance of mishaps, not least the frequent drenchings from rainstorms from which they were far less protected than travellers today. Judging from the writing, some diaries may well have been written on the journey itself, but most were probably written up during the evening or at leisure on the travellers' return from notes made at the time. One or two provide examples of beautiful penmanship and those of Lady Newdigate in 1747 (116, **566**) and the Rev Sir John Cullum in 1771 (96, **539**) deserve reproduction in facsimile. On the whole, the diarists paid little attention to the refinements of grammar and punctuation, and to preserve the character of the original diaries the extracts are printed here as written.

Compiling this book has given me a welcome opportunity to show in a practical way my gratitude for almost forty years in archive administration, during which time I have received nothing but help, courtesy and friendship from my erstwhile fellow county archivists and professional colleagues. Archivists experience as much stress in their work as other professionals, not least when those familiar 'circumstances beyond one's control' frustrate laudable plans for their offices and their personal aspirations, and the preparation of the book itself has not been without its anxieties. Even so, it will be obvious that the editorial work could not have been accomplished without tremendous practical help and encouragement from all quarters, particularly from the county archivists and their staffs, and from the expert guidance of Her Majesty's Stationery Office, to whom and to all others who have kindly assisted me I register my grateful thanks. Finally, the courtesy of the owners who have generously permitted extracts from their family diaries to be published is warmly acknowledged.

Robin Gard

March 1988

# Setting Out

*Every journey, whether long planned or hastily settled, was ever an adventure. The first, and often the most detailed, entries in many diaries reflect the nervous tension when, the bags packed, horses harnessed, farewells exchanged, the reins were touched and our observant traveller set his sights on the distant horizon and the journey ahead.*

'Give 'em their heads, Tom!'

1  Diary of Charles Brandling, 1834.  Northumberland Record Office,  ZBG.23

1

## A cheerful, if wet start, 1834

Left Losely on Friday the 18th July 1834 the party consisting of my Wife, my man & I & Martin P. who having an opportunity of laying aside for a few weeks his stationary Vocation in Gt. Russel St. & being withal an admirer of the Picturesque embraced the offer of a seat in our carriage. The Weather up to the day of our departure had been sultry & dry for several weeks, (with only one short interval) so that to the piscator a day or two's rain although at the outset of the Journey was by no means an unwelcome occurrence. Our first days drive was merely to Farnham. We dined & slept at Uncle Richards, Where it is unnecessary to add we were warmly received & lodged. The next mornings dawn was ushered in by torrents of rain, which it seemed had been pouring down during the whole night, & as we had now about 48 miles to accomplish (to Lyndhurst) before dark, our delight at the pouring of the heavens on the previous day, was somewhat checked. Nevertheless, knowing that "whatever is, is best" we exerted our ingenuity to avert the inconvenience from ourselves, & this we did by procurring some unbleached Rapia cloth, which for want of a better match we adjusted by hooks & eyes to the umbrella, & were thus in a great measure secured from the most pelting rain. In this way, we opened the eyes, & secured the grins of all the clodhoppers from Farnham to Winchester at which place we arrived about 3.

2    Diary of William Francis Lowndes Stone, 1834.    Oxfordshire Record Office,    LSN. VII/i/1    **(472)**

## Journey from Frampton in Gloucestershire to Craike in Yorkshire, 1812

| Towns | Inns | Miles | Fare | Driver | Gates | Time hr min |
|---|---|---|---|---|---|---|
| from F to Gloster | Kingshead | 10 | 0. 15. 0. | 0. 2. 6. | 0. 0. 8. | 1. 20. |
| to Tewkesbury | Hop Pole | 11 | 0. 16. 6. | 0. 2. 6. | 0. 1. 9. | 1. 35. |
| to Worcester | Star & Garter | 15 | 1.  2. 6. | 0. 3. 0. | 0. 2. 0. | 2. ½. |
| to Bromsgrove | Crown | 14 | 1.  1. 0. | 0. 2. 6. | 0. 1. 6. | 2. 10. |
| Birmingham | Hotel | 13 | 0. 19. 6. | 0. 2. 6. | 0. 1. 6. | 2. ¼. |
| to Sutton | 3 Tons | 8 | 0. 12. 0. | 0. 2. 6. | 0. 0. 6. | 1. ¼. |
| to Litchfield | Swan | 8 | 0. 12. 0. | 0. 2. 6. | 0. 0. 9. | 1 |
| to Burton | Kingshead | 13 | 0. 19. 6. | 0. 2. 6. | 0. 0. 9. | 1. ½. |
| to Derby | Kingshead | 11 | 0. 16. 6. | 0. 2. 6. | 0. 0. 9. | 1. ½. |
| to Alfreton | | 14 | 1.  1. 0. | 0. 2. 6. | 0. 1. 0. | 2 |
| to Chesterfield | Falcon | 10 | 0. 15. 0. | 0. 2. 0. | 0. 1. 3. | 1. ½. |
| to Sheffield | Tontine | 12 | 0. 18. 0. | 0. 2. 6. | 0. 1. 6. | 2 |
| to Doncaster | Old Angel | 18 | 1.  7. 0. | 0. 3. 0. | 0. 3. 0. | 3 |
| to Ferrybridge | Angel | 15 | 1.  0. 0. | 0. 2. 6. | 0. 2. 0. | 2. ¾. |
| to Tadcaster | White Horse | 12 | 0. 18. 0. | 0. 2. 6. | 0. 2. 0. | 2 |
| to York | Black Swan | 10 | 0. 15. 0. | 0. 2. 9. | 0. 2. 9. | 1. ¾. |
| to Craike | | 13 | 0. 19. 6. | 0. 2. 9. | 0. 2. 9. | 2 |
| | | 207 | 15.  8. 0. | 2. 3. 6. | 1. 6. 5. | 32 |
| | | | 2.  3. 6. | | | |
| | | | 1.  6. 5. | | | |
| | | | 4. 15. 3. | | | |
| | | | 23. 13. 2. | | | |

3   Gloucestershire Record Office,   D149/F215

## Notes of a tour through Kent in 1810

| [Miles] | |
|---|---|
| 15 | 19th July 1810 Leave Dartford thro' Gravesend, it being the best road, but a hilly stage to the *Crown* Inn *Rochester* a very clean one – three hours on this stage. |

Friday July 20th breakfast here. Total for tea, sleeping, horse & breakfast                                19s.6d

This Inn is a very good one but a most extravagant one.   at

2   nine o'clock go for *Chatham dock yard* – Sir Robt. the present

| | | |
|---|---|---|
| Commiss. – send our names & are admitted – the Impregnable a 90 gun ship to be launched the 1st of Augt.    to the person that showed her to us | | 2s.0d |
| The How of 130 guns, the largest ship as yet built, just on the stocks – to the porter attending us | | 2s.6d |
| Left gig at a little dirty public house in Brompton, a few hundred yards beyond the dock gates | | 1s.0d |

11 At 11 proceed thro' Brompton over the lines to the Sittingbourne Road & to *Rodmersham*

21st with Lushington at Rodmersham – ride over farm etc. 22nd servants                                                              5s.0d

At one o'clock to Canterbury, road rather hilly, to the King's Head Inn, Ridley, a very good one but very dear, at 4 o'clock Monday 23rd expences of dinner, breakfast etc.              £1.11s.0d

17 at 8 o'clock leave Canterbury for Margate 17 miles 2¾ hours, to the York Hotel – Wright, a good house, and situated to command a view of the pier, shipping etc.   expenses with turnpikes                                                              9s.6d

Map of Kent                                                              3s.0d

8 At three o'clock, the King's gate to the *London Hotel* – Page, at Ramsgate, – a tolerable road, rather difficult on account of cross roads. London Hotel not the best for visitors, as it does not look on the sea etc. The Kings Head – Bear, the better for this reason. Raffles                                                              10s.0d

> 4   Diary of Rev Townley Clarkson, 1810.   Cambridgeshire Record Office,   R57/11/1   (**42**)

## Distances travelled by 'every mode of conveyance' on a tour of North Wales and Ireland, 1813

Distance by every mode of conveyance

| | Miles |
|---|---|
| In the Gig with the Mare | 434 |
| Do. Post Horses | 162 |
| Do. Mr. Parke's Horse | 10 |
| In a Post Chaise | 55 |
| In the Mail | 25 |
| In a Heavy Coach | 27 |
| On Horseback | 111 |
| By Water (to Ireland) | 160 |
| In an Irish car | 65 |
| Total | 1049 |

And crossed 6 Ferrys

> 5   Diary of T J Parke and B Parke, 1813.   Northumberland Record Office, ZRI.31/2/7   (**458**)

# Travelling by post chaise, Isle of Wight, 1776

Septr. 3rd. at one in the afternoon embark'd for the Island, a very brisk gale, & rough sea, the Isle made a fine prospect before us, & to the right we saw the Needles & Hurst Castle; in one hour we were safely landed at Yarmouth, which is a poor place but one good Inn, & only one postchaise kept, which being gone out for the day, obliged us to stay till eight before we could set out for Newport, which is ten Miles, very stony road, & a great number of gates to open, but we made a very agreeable stage of it, by reading so long as our Candle lasted, & then singing, & repeating verses, arrived at Newport half past ten, at the Sun Inn, there is an exceedingly good Assembly room, it is a neat pretty town, the houses built of brick, the streets of a tolerable width, a square Market place, & good looking old Church . . .

6   Anonymous diary, 1776.   Isle of Wight Record Office,   81/98   (**326**)

6A   The Post Cart, J.A. Atkinson, c. 1840

## Conway ferries, 1790

The road then turns to the left & after crossing a beautiful neck of land brings you to

Conway Ferry. The river here is about a mile over. It was high water – very rough & the wind in our Teeth – I shall never forget the grand Appearance the Castle & Walls of Conway formed. They seemed entire two beautiful Hills covered with woodrise on each side – the river upwards appears an extensive Lake surrounded with a most romantic Country & on the other side opens into the Sea.

Lord L. had been at the ferry house all night. The Difficulty & Danger of getting his horses into the Boat determined us to ride up to another ferry which we were told was 4 miles off, tho we found the road very rough & long, missed our way, & had to enquire at a House where they spoke no English; yet the Beauty of the Country amply repaid us.

Tal Cafn Ferry is a good one. There is a float for Horses worked over by a rope & Pullies, but the tide had left it aground, so with some Difficulty we got them into a long Boat & went over in another. Two Horses of Ld B's had been sent hither, & going by whilst we were inquiring the road, had got over before us. As they were going over a vessel came down the River & the rope not being sufficiently slackened, it was caught by her Keels & drew the Capstern round with such violence . . . . .

7   Diary of William Cross, 1790.   Lancashire Record Office,   DDX 831/3/1 **(364)**

7A   Bramber Turnpike Gate, 1792.   Kent Archives Office,   W 2668   F1

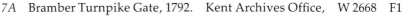

# Refreshment and a Safe Lodging

*With an arduous day ahead often requiring an early start, a hearty breakfast was needed to sustain the traveller whose mid-day appetite might be fortified only by a light luncheon packed in advance or hastily taken at a posting inn. A warm welcome and a substantial dinner at the end of the day were keenly anticipated, and compliments or brickbats to the genial or cross host are found in many diaries.*

# The Plume of Feathers tavern, near Carmarthen, 1804

August 12 Sunday. Set off for Carmarthen at half past six & in five minutes met a tremendous shower which lasted a short time and soon after, another; the weather continued wet and cold until we came to a House call'd Tavern spite, the sign of the Plume of Feathers nine miles from Carmarthen – here we breakfasted; stayed two hours . . . . .

8   Diary of Robert Parker FSA of Maidstone, 1804.   Hampshire Record Office,   18M51/557   (**263**)

9   The Plume of Feathers, on the road to Carmarthen, 1804.   Hampshire Record Office,   18M51/557   (**263**)

## A hearty breakfast at Bala, 1851

As a general rule the inns in North Wales are remarkably good and cheap, and the Lion at Bala certainly forms no exception to the rule. Our breakfast here consisted of grilled or fried and pickled trout, grilled ham and eggs, grilled mutton, roast beef and coquils, as good a glass of ale as I ever tasted and the indispensable 'cup that cheers but not inebriates'.

*10*    Diary of Richard G Francis, 1851.    Clwyd Record Office,    D/DM/538/1
     **(59)**

*11*    Clwyd Record Office,    DD/W7/5805

## Picnic with a packed lunch on the River Wye, 1824

We loitered about so long at (Goodrich Castle) that we did not reimbark till three o'clock, about 4 miles further down the river we stopped and dined in the boat just under the little village of Lidbrooke. We brought the provisions (consisting of a cold roasted leg of Lamb, bread and butter and Cheese, with bottled Perry, Cider and Ale) from the Inn at Ross, and the boatman got us some Water from a neighbouring Spring, & some slices of lamb broiled at a Gentleman's house by the water-side, who has the Iron and tin works on the spot – here is a Wharf for shipping coals to Ross & Hereford, with a railroad from the Collieries in the Forest of Dean. After we had paid a handsome Complement to our *provender* the Boatmen resumed their oars. I must not omit to mention that the indispensable utensils knives, forks, glasses and even a Table Cloth are sent with the refreshments
. . . . .

*12*    Diary of Phoebe Porter, 1824.    Hereford and Worcester Record Office, BA 3940/68(i)    **(281)**

## The Compton Arms, Stoney Cross, near Minstead, 1844

*View of the Compton Arms Inn – Stoney*
*april 16th 18*

*14*  Watercolour sketch by Lady Susan Holroyd, 1844.  East Sussex Record Office, Sheffield Place Records, 16

## Yorkshire hospitality, 1847

Just opposite this, on the Yorkshire side . . . is the diminutive thatched hamlet of Holwick. I know of no place in England where you will find a more primitive, a more hospitable or a happier class of people than the simple villagers in this seldom-visited retirement. This is a character I believe they have long retained, and I for one can gladly bear testimony to their genuine hospitality and freedom from many of the cold forms which sadly fetter society and so often cramp the better feelings and nobler sentiments of man; for a friend and I were overtaken here by fatigue: . . . . . . . and it was with no small pleasure that we dropped by the merest chance upon Holwick.

Knocking at the first door we came to, and stating our case, we were soon placed by a genial peat fire listening to the history of a groover's life. Not many moments elapsed before a large frying pan or bakestone was slung across the fire, and this was speedily graced by a famous cake thickly strewed with currants – in short we had a most capital tea. A hen was sitting upon a batch of eggs at one side of the fire, at the other ticked an ancient seven days' clock. A sharp-looking fair-haired girl of about 18 – the daughter of our host had actually, so he told us, officiated for some months as parish clerk, in the absence through illness of that important functionary of the established church. We smiled at the idea and I daresay looked somewhat incredulous, but to prove the statement true we were shown a book which had been presented by the minister for her services. On leaving to continue our march, by the light of a splendid moon, to Cotherstone, we had the utmost difficulty to obtain their acceptance of a small remuneration.

So much for their primitive simplicity and hospitality; – I will leave you to judge of their happiness when I tell you that there is in the village neither public-house, doctor, nor lawyer.

13   Diary of Francis P Cockshutt, 1847.   Durham Record Office,   D/X 36/5 **(139)**

## A night at the Raven Hotel, Shrewsbury, 1912

Headed along a level road, good surface. Rain steadily increased & about 5 miles out of Shrewsbury it came down in torrents. Nothing for it but to peg away. Cape kept worst off, but left side of breeches became soaked. Reached Lord Hill's column about 5 & splashed down into town & over English Bridge.

Now almost dark but policeman directed me to "Raven", a very first class house. Booked room & sent bike to garage. Went out & sent some postcards & bought paper. Then came back to my room, summoned chambermaid, sent coat & breeches to be dried, lit fire & rolled myself in eiderdown & sat in warm chair. Dried pants, stockings, shoes & contents of bag on fender. At last about 7.20 all things were dry & I dressed again & felt quite fit. Ran out & bought pair of felt slippers, washed & went down to 7.30 dinner.

About a dozen men in the room all in evening dress. Felt rather small & retired to side table. From the conversation, gathered that they were all army officers. Had very decent meal. Then with paper & pipe to smoking room. The officers all there, jawing, smoking etc. Breezey newcomer arrived & general conversation ensued. Gathered that manoeuvres or something were in progress. They were apparently all Staff men & not regimentals. Newcomer conducting examination of Territorial Officers or something. Tried to read paper but found their talk too interesting. They discussed the Balkan War where one of their friends had slipped out to serve. From that to Home Rule. Seemed anxious about the situation. Talked of civil war. Expressed desire to resign their commissions rather than fire on Ulstermen. Thought "Ancient Hibernians" a secret or "Jesuit" society & that "knifings" would be prevalent in consequence. Expressed violent hatred of Lloyd George & Winston Churchill. Doubted whether the Guards could be relied on in case of industrial trouble in London, but expressed confidence in the Line regiments. Related the treatment of a Socialist agitator by the 19th Hussars at Aldershot.

About 10.30 I retired & slept the sleep of the just & weary.

15   Diary of Philip Austin Leicester, 1912.   Hereford and Worcester Record Office,   BA8185/2(i)   **(307)**

# Country Towns

*Most travellers, whether on business or pleasure, necessarily stayed overnight in the principal country towns. While some hastened on early next morning, others had time to walk around the town and to observe its streets and public buildings, its shops and houses, its trades and occupations. Personal and instant impressions recorded in travel diaries may well note changes, capture a mood, or otherwise enliven the fixed picture presented by the timeless local history.*

## Colchester, 'much ruin'd in the late Civil Warrs', visited in 1672

The next day being the 21 we wrodd for Colchester a greate towne, but much ruin'd in the late Civil Warrs, the walls and severall churches beaten downe by greate shott. We saw the remnant of the Castle a square building with towers at each corner; it is now in the possession of that wretched fellow Sir John Norfolk, Serjeant to the House of Commons. We view'd the ruines of the Abby which was blowne up by the Kings party (upon their surrender of the towne to the Parlement) belonging then to the family of the Lucas's. Near to the Abby stands a small church wherein is inter'd Sir Charles Lucas who was shott to death upon the surrender of the towne in the late siege; there is put over him (by order of his brother the Lord Lucas) a stone with this inscription written in deepe ingraved characters that he was barbarously murder'd in cold blood by command of Sir Thomas Fairfax the General of the Parlament Army. He was shott under the walls of the Castle and the Royallists carry on a cheate (as the Papists did formerly) that the body works miracles and has left a remarke of divine vengeance on the ground where it was shott, noe grass ever growing since and remaining thus in the figure of a Cross. But a little boy told us that he had seen 'um poure scalding water upon it, therefore no wonder that it continued bare. Yet I cannot but think it strange that they should jugle at this rate to make saints of those that endeavour'd to overthrow the ancient liberties of the people of England. The chiefe trade of this place is the manufacture of bayes, extreamly decayed since the happy Restauration (as they call it).

16   Diary of John Walker, 1672.   Somerset Record Office,   DD/WHb
     3087   (502)

## Winchester, 'one of the sweetest and most healthy places in Europe', 1687

Fryday the 10th June 1687 . . . . . . . We came to Winchester safely about 7 of the Clock in the evening. We went to see first the Kings howse which was begun to be built by K.C. in the yeare 1683, it is on the side of the Hill to the west of the Town and is made in a half H very large and noble fitt for a Prince onely, it is built with brick and the corners and windows wrought with Portland stone, it is all Couverd with Lead. Since the late K$^s$ death it stands untouch'd but abundance of materials of all sorts lye ready there provided by the late K. There was design'd there very fine Gardens and a Parke and they bought in Land enough for them both cheifly of one Forder (whom the K design'd should be ranger). After the Kings howse we saw the Catherdrall, which is a very antient one   there is a dean and 12 Prebends   the Church is built of the same sort of Stone as Westminster Abby, There are abundance of remains of Popery to be seen there. The Bishop Dean & Prebends have all very good howses, and I know not a more pleasant quiet place for any Churchman than Winchester is. After this we went to see the Colledge founded by William of Wickam, There is a pretty Chappel & very good old painted Glasse Windowes, and a new School howse lately built extreamly pretty & convenient for that purpose They have a Warden underwarden and 10 Fellowes, and 60 or 70 Students, who are Chosen (when fitt) to New Colledge in Oxford. They have excellent Spring water in this Colledge in great abundance, and indeed the whole Town of Winchester is very well served with water, a River running through most of the Streets    Winchester is seated in a Bottom among the Hills and is one of the sweetest and most healthy places in Europe, I thinke to send my Sonne to School here. We lodged at the sign of the Chequer, a very good howse of Entertainment. . . . . . . .

Saturday June the 11th 1687. We came out from Winchester about 8 in the morning where the reckning came to about 30s.    a very good Inn and reasonable people.

17    Diary of John, later 1st Earl of Ashburnham, 1687.    East Sussex Record Office,    ASH 933    (**154**)

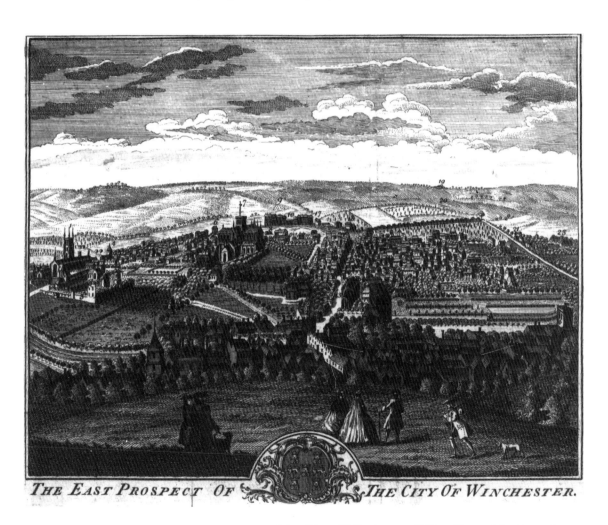

THE EAST PROSPECT OF THE CITY OF WINCHESTER.

18    East Prospect of the City of Winchester, 1750.    Hampshire Record Office,    Top. Winchester 2/5a

# Oxford in 1750

Dr. Ratcliff has left forty thousand pounds, to Build a new Library for the better disposition of the Books, its now Building, and its said to be done after a finer Plan than the Vatican at Room, or that at Paris; but I own by what I cou'd see of it I thought it seem'd to be a Heavy, Clumsey Building; tho' to be sure it will be a fine one when its finished.

The Printing House is removed from the Top of the Theatre where it formerly was, to a New one that was Built on the Profits of my Lord Clarrendons History, & call'd the Clarrendon Printing House, it is Built with Stone, and has an exceeding good Front North, & South, with Pillers of the Dorick Order.

The Museum is also a Handsome Building the Front to the Street is 60 Foot, it contains a Collection of Natural Curiositys, Roman Antiquities, & Medals, with Curious Agats, & other Stones: the particulers of wich tis impossible to remember: Here is the Skull of Oliver Cromwell; and a Mummy of great Antiquity.

19  Diary of William Mildmay, 1750.  Essex Record Office, D/DMy/15M50/1325 (**180**)

20  The Clarendon Building (then the Printing House), the Sheldonian Theatre, and the Ashmolean Museum, Broad Street, Oxford, by J. Donowell, 1757   Bodleian Library, MS. Top. Oxon. d. 36.fol. 97r.

## 'Vastly populous' Norwich, 1757

(28 July 1757). We reach'd Norwich that Evening passing thro' Aylesham, a small town 2 miles from Blickling. Norwich built in a circular form round a large high Hill, which is its centre, upon which stands the Castle, a square stone Building now converted into a Goal (sic). From this Hill we commanded the whole City which lay below us, surrounded by Hills at a small distance, from whence we may infer that the situation is damp and unwholesome. The Cathedral is saxon built, but has nothing extraordinary either in its Structure or Ornaments.

The Town vastly populous, employing an infinite Number of Hands in the Manufactory of Crapes & Stuffs, for which Norwich is famous. The whole country for many miles round are employed in preparing and spinning yarn for this M (anufactory). You see every woman and child almost with their wool fixt to the top of a stick carried in their Left Hand, which they draw out and twist with their Right without the use of a spinning wheel, or any other Instrument. The Town hall is a very fine Room, formerly a Church consisting of three Isles and two Rows of very neat Pillars, which have a grand Effect even in its present Use and Design. There are no less than thirty four Churches in the Town, too many for the Size of it, being not well endowed nor constantly served. Norwich Market is remarkable for the Quantity and Goodness of its Provision.

*21*   Anonymous diary, 1757.   Cornwall Record Office,   HL (2) 593   (**67**)

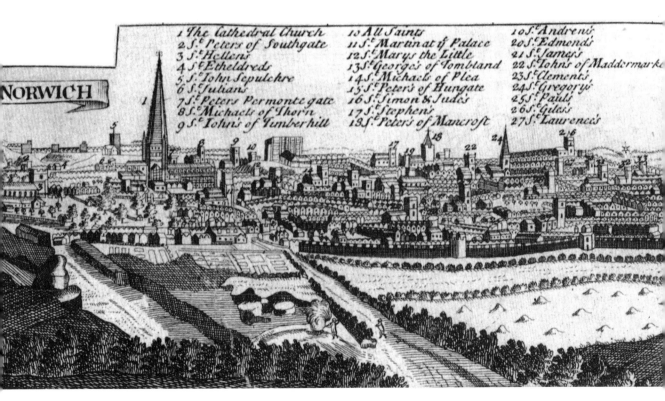

22   Norwich from the north east, 1757

# Berwick upon Tweed, 1760

Sunday, 13th July 1760.

The Town of Berwick is a pretty large town & has a large Bridge of 16 arches over the Tweed & is beautifully situated on the other side. The Town Hall is a good Building & has a Beautiful Turrett wch we took for the steple of the Church, And here the Bells are hung as the Church has no Steple. In the afternoon we saw the salmon fishing & saw ten taken at one draft: those of 20 inches & under are 6d apiece and are sold to Merchants of em in London and are called Gilses the Larger ones are all pick'd for London. This town has regular fortifications & there are very good Barracks for 2 regts.

23 Diary of George Thornhill, 1760. Cambridgeshire Record Office, Huntingdon, 148/5/274 (**48**)

24 High Street (Marygate), Town Hall and Main Guard, Berwick upon Tweed, 1799. John Fuller, *The History of Berwick upon Tweed*, 1799

26   View of Liverpool from the Bowling Green, by M A Rooker, 1770.

## A 'parade' around Liverpool, 1764

Thursday the 2nd of September we paraded Leverpool, & visited the new –
church called St Paul's, the Exchange, harbor & docks, with the new –
squares & chief streets. The new church is a very neat stone edifice, with an
handsome portico over the west door; the inside of which is a circular
dome, supported by Doric pillars, within the walls, which form a square.
The diameter of the dome is about fifty feet, & one side of the square is
about eighty feet. The altar also, & vestry are in recesses of about fifty feet
long, by fifteen wide. This church is not pewed but has benches with backs;
& the pulpit & desks are placed between two of the eastern pillars which
support the dome. Their town house is an elegant stone building adorned
with a neat cupola, & rich pediment embellished with emblematical figures
of trade & navigation supporting liberty & justice, in high relief; this is
supported by a double colonnade, where are spacious walks for the
merchants & tradesmen. Here are five or six wet & dry docks for unloading
& repairing ships, with several draw-bridges & floodgates, & inclosed by
large piers. In these lay some hundreds of vessels of different burthens from
most parts of the globe, which whilst we were admiring, together with the
florishing state of navigation in these parts; we had the pleasure of seeing a
Greenlandman & another ship in full sail up the river, & enter the harbor.
This town is in general pleasantly situated, & partly surrounded by the
Mersey; the middle parts of it are crowded with houses & narrow streets,
full of trade & inhabitants, but the markets are very commodious, & the
south east end of the town contains spacious & handsome squares &
streets, with neat new brick houses, inhabited by the genteeler sort of
merchants & tradesmen. Thus much for Leverpool; which we left on friday
Septr 3rd.

25   Anonymous diary, 1764.   Nottinghamshire Record Office,   M 380
   (**463**)

## Elegant Doncaster, 1773

September 15th. Went with Lord Balgoney to Doncaster, 4 miles distant.
The approach to the town very handsome between rows of trees, the fine
tower terminating the view. Cross a bridge over the Dun, navigable for
large barges. The streets very broad & well built. The market place spatious
& the retreates for the people elegant & supported by pillars; one is oblong;
the other round, both new.

The mansion house is elegant; the front adorned with corinthian pillars on
a rustic surbase; the green room a double cube, 21 yards by 11. The other
rooms good & convenient. The mayors reside here if agreable.

27    Diary of Thomas Pennant, 1773.   Warwickshire Record Office,
       CR.2017/TP2   (**582**)

28    Mansion House, Doncaster, 1804.   Edward Miller, *The History and
       Antiquities of Doncaster*, 1804/5.

# Taking the Waters

*Travelling in search of health became popular in the mid-eighteenth century and many diarists record the facilities, social life and entertainments available in Bath, Buxton, Cheltenham and other spas. By the end of the century sea-bathing had become equally fashionable, Weymouth and Brighton being patronised by the royal family. The origins and development of local seaside resorts may be traced in these diaries.*

## 'The varieties of Bath', 1766

Monday 24th Novbr – There was a charity breakfast at the rooms, at which were present 700, but we not being charitably inclined took a snug breakfast at home, after which we sally'd into town to provide ourselves with tea, coffee, sugar and all other requisites relative to house-keeping and after this business was finished we returned back and received a morning visit from Doctr Hays and Mr.Cumberbach. Dined at half an hour past two o'clock. In the evening we went to the play-house where was very well performed The Clandestine Marriage with the farce of Thomas and Sally – NB. The present theatre is under Mr.Simpson's ballroom, that in Orchard Street not being as yet entirely repaired and enlarged according to the manager's design, and may be called a neat play-house for its size . . .

Monday 8th [Dec] Visited the Pump-room, returned home to breakfast after which Mr.Giffard rode out with Mr.Browne; we dined at Lady Halkerton's and in the evening were entertained with fire-works. After tea, went to Mr.Derick's Benefit Ball with Lady Arundel, drank tea in the Rooms with Mr.Read, played at cards with Lady Edwards and Lady Charleville and returned home at half an hour after ten o'clock. Such are the varieties of Bath!

29 Diary of Elizabeth Giffard, 1766–1767.   Clwyd Record Office,   D/NH/ 1074   (**54**)

31   The Pump Room, Bath, c.1800.

# The Duke of Kingston's Baths, 1766

Friday 26th Dec. . . . we afterwards took a walk to the Circus to see
Mr.Gainsborough's paintings with which we were very much pleased.
From thence our curiosity led us to take a survey of the Duke of Kingston's
Baths, which, after some years labour, are now entirely compleat, at the
expence, they say, of £5000 – they are situated directly over the old Roman
Baths and divided into three apartments, each entirely separate and
consisting of a waiting room for a servant, a chamber with a fire place for
the patient to undress, dress in etc., and a neat octogon building with a
cupola in a recess of which is the Bath, lined with white glazed Dutch tyle
and supplied from a spring of its own. These Baths are filled in about three
minutes and there is a pipe of luke-warm water to allay the heat, if too
great, and cocks to throw the water on any part of the body. Behind is a
place called the vapour-room where the steam from each of the three is
conveyed and where patients sometimes are advised to sit and in a few
minutes are thrown into a violent profusion of sweat. The conveniency of
these Baths is great as the Water is quite fresh and you are not subject to
any gazer and are accommodated with every necessary with the greatest
propriety – but the expence is considerable, five shillings being each time
paid to the use of His Grace of Kingston.

30  Diary of Elizabeth Giffard, 1766–1767.  Clwyd Record Office,  D/NH/
1074  (**54**)

32  The North Parade, Bath, c.1800.

## Sidmouth in 1797

From Exeter I proceeded to Sidmouth, the place of my destination, fifteen miles distant, to dinner: the roads rough but the views interesting. The place from its low situation on the beach is sheltered and warm it being surrounded on every side except towards the sea by high hills; the pleasantness of its situation of late years has attracted many bathers though its beach is by no means so well adapted to the purpose as a more shelving sandy shore, it being a bank of shingles or large pebbles and the sea deep and at times very rough near the coast. At present there are but a four machines employed and the gentlemen and ladies engage them indiscriminately. To remedy in some measure the inconvenience of the loose beach the inhabitants have formed a gravel walk nearly a quarter of a mile in length facing the sea which is the usual resort for the company also a thatched building to shelter them in bad weather and a billiard table. They have besides a spacious assembly and card room, where they meet six evenings in the week during the season which are in general well attended, the subscription being half a guinea and two shillings on coming into the room on a ball night. The accommodations at the London Inn are good and the people civil.

33  Diary of Rev John Skinner, 1797.   Somerset Record Office,   DD/SAS C/1193/10  (**507**)

## George III and the Royal Family at Weymouth, 13, 14 August 1805

13.  The dear good and gracious king arrived at five o'clock this morning, the queen and princesses some time after; they retired to rest soon after for a few hours; his Majesty immediately went into a warm sea bath on his arrival; at 10 o'c[lock] he was at the camp to view the troops; his Majesty came past our lodgings to the pier before dinner, and after at the camp again a feu de joie was fired and every ship fired a royal salute; it was beyond all description grand, it affected me very much as well as my son; it must be something like an engagement.
14.  Sunday, the royal family all were at church; afterwards they, king and princesses, walked down the esplanade to the pier, the queen did not walk. Between 7 and 8 o'c[lock] the royal family all walked on the esplanade and after to the rooms, where we went, and highly gratified we were at seeing them enter, the queen's German band playing 'God Save the King'; a part of the room enclosed by a silk cord where the royal family enter, and every body who has been introduced stand within the cord to converse with them, other people stand on the outside the cord and have an opportunity of hearing the conversation; the band keeps playing during the royal family stay in the room, which in general is an hour; his Majesty's eyes appear very indifferent, always wore a green shade over them; he seemed in good spirits, talks a great deal; the queen and princesses looked in good health excepting the Princess Amelia who is delicate; Princess Elizabeth looks lively and good-humoured, she is very lusty; The Duke of Cambridge a most elegant looking man, a most pleasing countenance; The Duke of

Cumberland tall and genteel but not handsome, he has lost an eye. The royal family did not remain so long as usual, as the king's eyes were so indifferent; we stayed tea and walked about the room for some time after they left, the band playing all the time

34   Diary of Abigail Gawthern, 1805.   Nottinghamshire Record Office, M 23,904   **(464)**


## Cheltenham, 1814

Cheltenham, the Plough Inn dirty, but otherwise the accommodation good & not so exorbitantly dear as might be expected at a watering place. The George is a good Inn, but not so much used by the better sort of people as the Plough. Stabling at the Plough good & standing for carriages, but no lock up coach houses. Lodgings are to be had at every shop in the town & a great many houses are built in the outskirts for the accommodation of families, but it is advisable to take one on the south side of the town for the purpose of being nearer the wells. Cambray, Bath Villas, Montpelier Place are most convenient for that reason, as well as being best adapted for the reception of families from the interior arrangements. Carts with Donkeys in them are provided at 1s. 8d. per hour, & Donkeys at 1s. for those who cannot walk to the Wells. The hour of going to the Wells in the morning for the water is from 7 till ½ past nine. Those most in use at this time are the Montpelier belonging to Mr Thompson. There are several subscription library's, but Henneys is the best. Assembly Rooms & theatres. . . . . . . . . One of the prettiest rides is thro' Leckhampton, Sultrington to the Gloucester turnpike, from Frog Mill & then home by the Bath Road. There is a new turnpike making from the end of Portland Street to Evesham, 17 miles, which when finished will be a great convenience to the residents of that place & Cheltenham, as in going from one place to another at present there is no road but round thro' Tewkesbury.

35   Diary of Sir Matthew White Ridley, 1814.   Northumberland Record Office,   ZRI.32/3/8   **(459)**


## The Prince Regent's Brighton, 1818

On the 21st of May 1818, we left our residence in Charter House Square in a Carriage and four, for Miss Lane's Villa Bedford Row Brighton, this place is very large and is enlivened during some part of the Summer by the Prince Regent's residing at the Pavillion which is now being considerably enlarged and ornamented, apparently in the Chinese Style. Provisions are very plentiful here, there is a market for everything that is necessary for life and pleasure. The bathing does not appear to be very good, for the descent into the Sea is so rapid, as to preclude the possibility of pushing the machines in deep enough to jump into the Sea. The Chalybeat is situated near the Sea, the water is not very strong and as they charge 6d. per glass I imagine that they have not much custom. Packets sail every day from this place to Dieppe, wind and weather permitting, great numbers of People go by them, one that we saw land brought 24 passengers besides dogs, parrots and other animals, which combined with the sickness under the influence of which they all suffered, rendered it almost impossible for them to walk to the Inn. The Prince's statue in the Crescent is going to decay very fast having lost one hand and being otherwise . . . . . . .

36  Diary of Frances Sayer, 1818.  East Sussex Record Office,  SAY 3394 (**162**)

View of Brighton opposite the Grand Parade, by Frances Sayer, 1824. East Sussex Record Office,  SAY 3394 (**162**)

## Cromer in 1821

On an eminence near the town there is a light-house, and a new Jetty has lately been built, which makes a very pleasant walk. The sands at low tide are very smooth and firm, and are well adapted for walking and riding, or driving. . .

We used to dine together at Tucker's Inn, which is the principal Inn in Cromer, and the Master of it is nearly King of Cromer. Our dinner hour was 4 o'clock. We used to have plain dinners and we did not drink wine except on Sundays. We separated at 5, and I used generally to play at Billiards or walk on the jetty. There was a public Billiard Room (from which you had a very good view of the sea), at which you paid 3d per game, and 6 for a Love Game, and it was usual to play five games, and then to give up the Table, if any persons were waiting to play.
During the early part of my residence there was little Gaiety going forward, but Sir Jacob Astley, who has a house at Melton about 14 miles from Cromer, came here with his family and excited the people to have some Balls. We had 3 dances at the Reading Room, and one grand Ball at Tuckers at which Sir Jacob was one of the Stewards.

37  Diary of John Thornton, 1821.  Northamptonshire Record Office, Th 3183  (**446**)

## Cromer from the Lighthouse, 1825

38   Diary of Mr Marten, 1825.   Norfolk Record Office,   MC 26/1 5044 x
**(396)**

## Pegwell village and Ramsgate Baths, 1821

The little Village of Pegwell is very beautiful. The Cottages are all elegant
and picturesque and it looks peaceful & happy. Here is a public House
called Belle Vue and it well deserves its name for on walking through the
House into the Tea Gardens which are at the very edge of the Cliff you have
a most delightful view of the surrounding Country & close to you is the Sea
running into the Bay. Returning home we stopped at the Warm Baths
which are very handsome and well furnished. The Baths are of Italian
Marble, the Dressing Rooms have a pretty little fireplace, two chairs, a small
Sofa table, and a carpet, over which is a piece of Scarlet Cloth on which you
walk to the bath. Mama & Aunt Fanny bathed. The reading room is
between the Gentlemen & the Ladies baths, and it is a very handsome
building. We returned to Tea.

39   Diary of Frances Sayer, 1821.   East Sussex Record Office,   SAY 3396
**(163)**

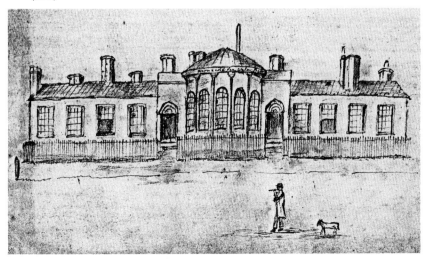

## Holiday in Margate and Ramsgate, 1839

August 1st. After breakfast, came in Royal William Steam Packet to Margate – very fine day – enjoyed it very much till within twenty miles when both Bernard & I felt very ill & had a touch of sea sickness. To the Duke's Head Hotel, pleasantly situated. After sitting still an hour, walked on the Cliff beyond the Fort where are some very pleasant lodgings & good sea views & afterwards on the Pier which is a very pretty one & where a good Band of Wind Instruments were playing. After tea to several Bazaars, Boulwards Library where were Raffles & Mime going on & Crowds of people everywhere.

August 2nd. Walked on Marine Parade &c & came in an open Car to Ramsgate, a beautiful drive by the Sea all the way through Kingsgate by the North Foreland, Broadstairs & drove to the Royal Oak & called on Mrs Martins who went with us a little while about lodgings. Engaged some at Miss Barratts, 6 Plains of Waterloo, one sitting room with Bow-window Balcony & Veranda & 2 bedrooms, one a double bedded room, for 2 guineas & a half a week. Sat on the Sands & walked on the Pier, took dinner at the Inn & came for tea to the lodgings.

August 3rd. Mr S & Bernard bathed in the morning & we were on the Sands a great deal. Called on Mrs Martins & in the evening walked on the West Cliff & heard the Band play, it (being) very fashionable Promenade time & numbers of people.

40   Diary of Eliza Spurrett, 1839.   Leicestershire Record Office, 7D54/2/3   (374)

41   Margate, c.1839   Kent Archives Office

# The Beauties of England

*Tourists have ever been attracted by the distant scene,
particularly of mountainous and natural landscapes. Thus, the
Lakes, the Peak District, and the West Country were popular
from the late eighteenth century, though the Isle of Wight, Kent
and Sussex feature a little later. However, the gentler scenery
and subtler beauties of Southern England, the Midlands and
East Anglia were savoured by fewer tourists, while mid-Wales,
the Pennines, the Yorkshire Dales and Moors, Northumberland
and the North generally were seldom visited.*

# The Peak Cavern, Castleton, 1765

. . we came to Castleton, a pretty large village at the head of a pretty well enclosed valley, a few hundred yards to the westward of this town is the shivery Mountain one of the wonders of this peak, this Hill is said to shiver constantly down without being less which I apprehend is a mistake, at the summit of these adjoining hills are the ruins of an Old Castle, we now 5 of us entered the D. . .l A. .se hole, the height of the Entrance of the precipice is 37 yards, from here to the first river 150, from hence to the 2(nd) River 70, betwixt the first and 2nd water is a Cavity 70 yards wide & 20 high, the next place of note is called the Devils cellar, from the Devils cellar to the Swallow, from the Swallow to the Arches, from the Arches to tom of Lincoln, from tom of Lincoln to the furthest end, making in the whole length 750 yards, it is here 207 yards Deep from the Summit, about 220 yards in you have a mighty curious place called the chancell where some Boys climb up and sing, about 3 miles from here is a place called Perryfoot where is a large Swallow supposed to take in the water that makes its way out at this wonderful place, it is supposed their are more cavities further up this water if they could be come at, there are several little houses at the Entrance inhabited by people who make whipcord &c, here are also many curious things petrified by the mineral water which drops & trickles down the sides of this most curious limestone rock, I forgot to observe that we were ferried over Stix by means of a Boat and crossed it twice more by resting upon 2 men's shoulders each supporting a thigh, we sometimes ascend sometimes descend now go upright then creep afterwards sideways & last of all wade for a long way together . . . . we lodged at the sign of the Castle in Castleton where we made a hearty repast upon Mutton chops & Oat Cake but a very cross Landlady.

42  Diary of George Culley, 1765.   Northumberland Record Office, ZCU./1 **(451)**

43  View of the Peak Cavern, from *The Modern Universal British Traveller*, Derbyshire Record Office, D3699/2p 89.

## Exeter Cathedral from Mount Wear, 1788

The View here seen, was taken from the Eminence called Mount Wear, adjoining to the Bridge of Countess Wear, and at the distance of two miles from Exeter. This sketch exhibits one of the specimens, which all the Environs of Exeter possess of the Richness, the fertility, the picturesque scenery of the Country. The vicinity of few Cities hath such decorations of Wood, water & Villa's as this is adorned with. The hedge-rows of fine Elms, saving to the West, where the descent is rapid and open to the River, prevent the city from being seen, and the only object that is beheld, is the magnificent Cathedral, towering high over the summit of the trees, and affording an august spectacle to all the surrounding country. The rural scenes in front of the road, the cottage, the river, a Paper-mill and the woody inclosures form a most pleasing picture, which is strikingly embellished by the grandeur of the Cathedral, and by the distant back ground of Halldown.

*44*   Diary of Rev John Swete, 1788.   Devon Record Office,   MS 2   (**111**)

*45*   Exeter Cathedral from Mount Wear, by Rev John Swete, 1788.   Devon Record Office,   MS 2 (**111**)

# Dunster Castle and Village in 1796

But a little way now remained to the town of Dunster, the suburbs of which lay low, shadowed by the woods, which spread themselves from the base of the Castle Mount to the conical top which was crested with firs. Having rode through the whole of a long street at the Westernmost extremity I reached the Inn – a large old House, whose sign was the arms of the Lord of the Castle – from hence the prospect of this ancient and vast Pile, proudly perched on the Northern side of the more elevated mound, or Keep, was uncommonly good. Rising from the thick bosom of surrounding woods, it exhibited itself as the strong bulwark of the subjacent town; its massy walls and embattled towers recalled to memory the feudal times in which it had been erected. . . . . .

From a Window of the Inn, while my dinner was getting ready I took the opposite sketch over the Houses, of the chief street and the North-west fronts of the Castle – the frame of the drawing is that which included the Window, and the extent of the View, such as was comprised by the aperture at a table's distance. From another sitting room up stairs, with an Eastern Aspect, the Views were of a champaign country seen over the groves of Dunster, a long extent of flat coast extending Eastwards towards Watchet, and more inwards the rising country about Carhampton.

46   Diary of Rev John Swete, 1796.   Devon Record Office,   564M/F12
     (**115**)

47   Dunster Castle, watercolour by Rev John Swete, 1796.   Devon Record
     Office,   564M/F12   (**115**)

# The romantic scenery of Shanklin Chine, 1817

Of all the lovely morning views I ever saw, I think this was the most beautiful. A slight breeze ruffled the waves, which glittering in the sun, dazzled the eye, attempting to gaze. On all sides surrounded with the romantic scenery of Shanklin Chine, which is a chasm in the Cliff, feathered to the bottom, with stunted trees of various descriptions, down whose centre rushes a small but noisy brook, which by some is supposed to have worked the fissure in the Cliff. Cottages here and there interspersed in the most picturesque & romantic style, relieved the Landscape. We descended by a path chiefly of steps to the Beach, where, when we had satiated ourselves with looking up at the Chine, we amused ourselves by looking about among the rocks for ammonites & fossils which might have fallen from the mass of Rock above. Not being prepared for such an expedition, we had no implement to break the mass of fossil shells, which we found in great abundance . . . I however made a small collection of petrified wood & some masses of fossil shell which you may better know the merits of than myself.

*48*  Diary of George Crewe, 1817–1818.  Derbyshire Record Office, D2375M/180/23  (**106**)

*49*  Shanklin Chine, by William Cooke, *A New Picture of the Isle of Wight*, 1808.

# 'The picturesque little port' of Boscastle, 1866

Wellington Hotel, Boscastle – a new, large and well appointed house.

Tuesday, 2nd October.
Feeling somewhat lazy, strolled out to see the place – a straggling little town of many mean dwellings, built entirely of slate – a country of slate – houses, walls, everything built of it. The Harbour, the queerest & most picturesque little inlet imaginable, formed by a double re-entering angle – how vessels can get in seems a mystery – rocks everywhere and a sea which even in calm weather surges heavily in, but when accompanied by a groundswell – in spite of two breakwaters – is so insecure an anchorage that vessels have to be restrained by enormous hawsers to save them from destruction. At low water a singular spectacle is exhibited of a jet of water which is at intervals ejected with a loud report at the same time that a column of spray & water is discharged to a considerable distance – as if expelled from a steam pipe. This is due to the passage of the sea through a fissure by which the rock is perforated – the folks call it 'the blower'. In the course of my ramble I made my way to the foot of an awful black chasm – fearful the violence with which the sea hurls itself against these crags! and, then, the hoarse rattle of the merciless undertow . . . . .

Friday, 5th October
Quitted my comfortable quarters at Boscastle for Penzance. After breakfast, strolled down again to the picturesque little port which has been likened by some to Balaclava on a small scale. Enormous hawsers lie about the piers as thick as a man's thigh – yet such is the force of the groundswell at times that a vessel moored by three of them has been known to have had all three snapped as though they had been so much pack thread.

*50* Diary and sketch by Sir William Guise, 1866.   Gloucestershire Record Office,   D326 F50   (**244**)

Membury Castle.

## Seaton and Axmouth in 1872

Having satisfied our curiosity on this front, we proceeded to the hills overlooking the Axe. We went through a field to Seaton Down, and looked at the earthworks, returning by the field, where we saw only two or three sling-stones, one very large. Thence we journeyed south towards Seaton, but turned into a field to have our luncheon, for we were hungry and thirsty, and it was very warm.

When we were on the beach, we saw the cone of Membury Castle, distant, as they said, nearly 12 miles, crowned with trees, rising towards the north – as per rude sketch.

We examined the great mound, on which a fort was built to keep off pirates. I made it 150 paces in diameter, and Mr Herneker made it 25 feet high. They say it was once 20 feet higher. The esplanade is now carried over it.

From this place we went to the river and crossed by the ferry.

e mound of the old Fort, on the beach, looking towards the west.

erry-house, warehouse, Haven cliff, and mouth of Axe river.

*51* Diary of Peter Orlando Hutchinson, 1872. Devon Record Office

# The Lakes

*Considering the poor roads in this remote area of the country at the time, it is remarkable how many tourists explored the Lake District in the late eighteenth and first half of the nineteenth centuries – most of the sixty or so diaries recording such tours belong to this period. The combined effect of unfamiliar expanses of water, backed by precipitous mountains with rocky cliffs, cascading falls, and brooding peaks forever cloud-topped, excited the traveller with feelings of awe and wonder. Not without danger did the intrepid tourist venture over high passes into unfrequented dales, though few dared to climb on to the fells.*

## Derwentwater from Castle Crag, 1797

In the evening I went up Castle Crag above Keswick where from the height of the rock, the whole map of Derwentwater may be perfectly discovered and eight Islands plainly perceived there is a ninth not easily distinguished from this spot and Lords island looks smaller than Vicars from this point. I endeavoured to discover any traces of the Roman fort or the Castle of the Radcliffs but though I ascended the hill with the enthusiastic eye of an antiquary I could find nothing on which to vent my conjectures or the least remnant of a foundation which from its reputed strength I would not have supposed so completely destroyed.

52    Diary of Sir William Gell, 1797.    Cumbria Record Office, Barrow, Z293    (**100**)


## 'The whole map of Derwentwater', 1797

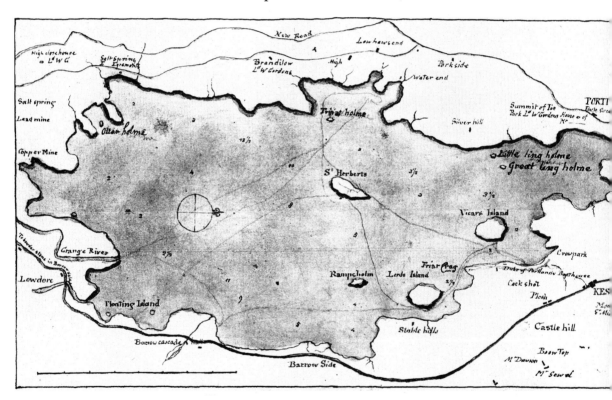

53    Diary of Sir William Gell, 1797.    Cumbria Record Office, Barrow, Z293    (**100**)

## Sweet Mary of Buttermere, 1805

(Mary Robinson of Buttermere was a noted Cumberland beauty who was married under false pretences by the imposter and forger, John Hatfield; she was afterwards commemorated in song and story).

We were civilly recd. by Mary who informed us that as we were the third party come to dine at the inn we must unavoidably wait for our dinners till they had all dined when she would do the best in her power for us . . . . after dinner we went accross the cromack water which is about ½ a mile from the inn on the other side we were amused by seeing some men fishing arriving just at the time the net was drawn. Took a row a little way down the lake & returned to be soon after which Mary prepared us a supper which consisted chiefly of honey & milk for this place being near 10 miles from a market & much resorted to at this time of year little choice remains to those travellers who do not come soon after market day. Here we slept & our accomodation was tolerably comfortable . . . . poor Mary Robinson attracted much interest with us from her affecting history, & her civil & diffident behaviour to all guests raised her high in our estimation. In the parlour in which we sat were the following lines inscribed with a diamond on the window, for had they been with less permanent materials her modesty would have made her long since efface them for we could trace not a word of the sort in any other part of the house:

> "The sigh from thy bosom discard
> Sweet Mary of Buttermere vale
> Thy sufferings will meet with reward
> When Angles once hear of thy tale
>                31st of Aug. 1803".

*54*  Anonymous diary, c.1805.   Cumbria Record Office, Barrow, BDX/59/2 (**102**)

## The wilds of Borrowdale and Grange Village, 1804

Wednesday July 4th. In the morning we took Huttons boat, and landed at Lowdore. Thence we walked into the wilds of Borrowdale. The road is very narrow, and is skirted above on the left hand, by stupendous precipices; down which huge fragments of rock have tumbled from time to time, and

border each side of the way in terrible confusion. The river Grange glides on the right; and at the same side, the narrow vale is enclosed by huge barren mountains. Castle Crag, which to persons sailing on the Lake appears to stretch its foot into the waters, now retires into the dale, and seems to mock pursuit. At the distance of about a mile from Lowdore opens a charming view of the small and simple village of Grange, which is one of the sweetest retirements I ever beheld.

*55* Diary and sketch by Rev W Shepherd, 1804.   Cumbria Record Office, Barrow,   Z198   (**101**)

## Pic-nic on Ullswater, 1844

At Patterdale almost a new Inn has sprung up since my last visit last year, with very nice gardens & lawn before it. Taking boat we embarked on what I cannot help calling the grandest of the lakes. The mountains rising as it were from the bottom of the waters. Had a very uninteresting boy to row us – not only ill-favoured but loutish & stupid – like many of these north country bumpkins. Landed in Gowbarrow Park, had a capital pic-nic on the banks of the Lake, and no Sir Gregory Grumpy to warn us off for daring to grease his grass.

*56* Anonymous diary, 1844.   Lancashire Record Office,   DDX 1282/4 (**370**)

# A drive through Lakeland, 1844

Saturday morning brought most lovely weather with it, and so after breakfast we started off for Langdale Pikes. Passing Skelwith Bridge & Force, or Waterfall, Elterwater, Blea Tarn, and Little Langdale, we at length arrived at a farm house called Milbeck, situated in a most romantic valley. The road from Ambleside very rough and precipitous, winds round the mountains, and is in many places so narrow that it seems a miracle that carriages can travel over it in safety. We drove in some style in a two horse car, with postilion in a yellow jacket, round hat, &c, and overtook a gentleman driving his own four wheel carriage & horses, with his wife – his man servant riding the leader. He appeared to run some risk in venturing without a guide but we had the felicity of seeing him arrive safe at the Inn an hour after us. The Pikes are very lofty, 2000 & odd feet, and very barren. After a very homely lunch of bread & cheese, ale & milk which was furnished at 6d. a head, we toiled up to Dungeon Gill, and found it like the rest of the Cascades – rather in want of water.

57 Ullswater and Rydal Water, c. 1840. Lancashire Record Office, DDX 1282/4 (**370**)

# Wales

*Most of the fifty or so diaries recording visits to Wales date between 1770 and 1850. The mountains and the natural landscape were the principal attractions – climbing Snowdon was a popular, and indeed well catered for, activity – with the additional interests of romantic scenery, ruined abbeys and castles, marine pleasures, and a sense of being in a foreign land, which strange customs and the Welsh language accentuated.*

## Swansea in 1773

From Neath we had a pleasant ride to Swansea having our views diversified with several outlets between the hills towards the Sea. As we approached the ferry we passed by some very large Copper works (there are others in and about the Town – the Copper ore all comes from Cornwall) belonging to Mr. Morris. One inconvenience sttends them by which Swansea suffers very much which is a perpetual Smoke, that is found very disagreeable even to those who are only to stay a short time in the town. The Town is neat but not so large as Cardiff. The Castle has some very curious remains left, particularly the little arches turned under the battlements, probably in order to give lightness and strength to the work – it is now used as a poor house. The Chief Magistrate is a portreeve under the D. of Beaufort (The D. of Beaufort owns this Castle, Monmouth, Ragland, Mumbles, etc). The harbour is commodious for ships of considerable burthen.

*58*  Diary of Luttrell Wynne, 1773.  Cornwall Record Office,  PD 469  (**74**)

*59*  Sketch of Swansea by Luttrell Wynne, 1773.  Cornwall Record Office, PD 437

## Welsh costumes, 1822

. . . the women have clean frilled caps tied under their chins and wear over these a man's hat of felt or coarse beaver and have shoes and stockings black worsted, in general the rest of their dress nothing uncommon – clothes very neatly put on – the men wear what my father called slop frocks like loose great coats cut short . . .

*60*   Diary of Sarah Brinkley, July–August 1822.   Clwyd Record Office, DD/PR/133   **(61)**

ERRAND GIRL     FARMER'S DAUGHTER     MARKET WOMAN     WINTER COSTUME     LLANARTH GIRL

*61*   Welsh Costumes, from *Catherall's Picturesque Views in North Wales*, by T Catherall, c.1860.   Clwyd Record Office

## The Mawddach Valley, July 1813

The Valley from Dolgelley to Barmouth is singular and beautiful, and perhaps has more character than any Valley in the Kingdom. For the first two miles it continues to possess the same features as distinguish it from its commencement at Drwsynant; a river, fertile meadows, extensive woods, and the rugged crags of Cader Idris. From the junction of the Mawddach, not far from the remains of Cimmer Abbey, now an uninteresting Ruin, the Valley exhibits a tame continuity of meadows, separated by banks &

ditches & intersected by the river which here receives the tide, for about two miles. It then breaks into wooded hills & promontaries projecting into the estuary, each as it is passed presenting the landscape in a different point of view. The roads winds between the base of the mountains on the right & these, which at times suspend the prospect only to restore it with new & varied effect. In this way nearly three miles are passed, when the estuary assumes the appearance of a large Lake surrounded by lofty mountains. The road cut in the side of the mountain, traverses the verge of this expanse considerably above, & almost overhanging its surface, for about two miles & a half, till the town of Barmouth arrests your progress. This is beyond comparison the most delightful ride we have met with. It is only less beautiful in returning to Dolgelley, as the hills & promontaries then present to the eye fronts more deficient of wood than in the progress down the Valley. But probably a birds-eye view of the whole, which is obtained from a break on the top of one of the mountains that overhangs the Lake, may be deemed the most enchanting of all. The Valley is here laid before you as it were on a Map with all its lines & points of beauty, & the magnificent heads of Cader Idris & the distant Arrans forming a boundary, make up a landscape not to be surpassed in any part of Great Britain.

62   Diary of T J Parke and B Parke, 1813.   Northumberland Record Office,   ZRI.31/2/7   (**458**)

63   Cader Idris and head of Mawddach Valley, mid-19th century. Gwynedd Archives Service, Dolgellau.

## Pystyll y Mawr Vach Falls, 1860

Here we struck down amongst the brushwood, on emerging from which, the Fall burst suddenly upon us, & it was beautiful. This sketch I made, Sophy & Lechmere up on the rock before the Fall, Gertrude down on her knees, drinking, Katey, Mary & I in the foreground. The water runs through quantities of small rocks, with shingly sort of shores. It comes dashing gloriously down from the height all in foam, looking so clear & bright, & in the shadows, just varying in tint according to the colour of the rocks it flows over. When we had taken a good look at the Fall, we rose to go; and was packing up my sketching things, I heard a shout of "Oh! such a pretty little cave!" & there it was, not far from where we had been sitting, the entrance to a little cave in the side of the hill, almost buried in the luxuriant fern & heather that grew round the entrance. Right before the mouth, the water dripped constantly like a sparkling veil, so plentifully that we could only just see inside. We all looked in, but could see nothing. Here is the sketch, with me in the foreground, & Katey looking over my shoulder.

*64*   Diary of Frederica St John Rouse-Boughton, 1860.   Bedfordshire Record Office,   OR 2244/5   **(25)**

## Snowdon lifts her veil, 1865

Suddenly in a moment to the admiration of all the clouds fled and Snowdon uncovered her head like a dainty maiden lifting her vail and displayed the most stupendously gorgeously beautiful view I ever saw formed before my eyes: like a fairy scene the lakes and rivers and the distant sea on the west and north west seemed to be mirrors for the swallows, standing out like silver among the rugged mountains on every side and the peaks of rock like volcanos crowned with smoke seemed to be supporting the gouse vail of mists on their giant shoulders on purpous to give us unworthy mortals a peep into the happy lands of eternity, the spurs and sides of Snowdon were now and again tipped with gold by the rays of the sun which shot through the openings of the mists as they scud along, tracing their way as if led by the hand of Iris along the precipitous sides of that Olympus: the roaring torrents on the north side echoed like continued thunder up that side of the mountain which is 15 hundred feet in the perpendicular and the stillness of the mind for the moment and the awful grandeur seemed to portray the presence of the Almighty himself and the omnipotency of him by whom all things were made; after the first murmur of admiration we all stood for a few seconds as if over-powered by the lovelyness of the panorama before us and then they with one accord poured thanks upon me . . . as if I had actually brought it to pass and had (as one said) "like an angel cleft the clouds with a smile" and had introduced the coy Snowdon to the heaving Phoebus (I think he must have been in love or a poet perhaps from his appearance) However I only wish Phoebus had kept up his flirtation longer and made use of his opportunities for we had only time to devour the view which extended on one side over the Llanberis pass to Moel Llewellin mountain 3462 high on the North, to the high lands of Anglesea on the West and the St. Georges channel and Cader Idris and the Berwin Range on the South and the celebrated vale of Llangollen on the East shewing nigh

66   The Summit of Snowdon, by J. Brandard, mid-19th century.   Dyfed
     Archives Service,   Castell Gorfod Colln, 307

twenty lakes and nearby two thousand sq. miles of country when suddenly fair Snowdon blushed with the last words of Phoebus and a white mist wet and cold with a chill wind in a moment surrounded us and a fleeting second shut out the heavenly vision like a dissolving view beneath our feet;

*65* Diary of A S Gulston, 1865. Dyfed Archives Service, Derwydd H 26 (**151**)

## Festiniog and Welsh customs, 1868

Finally we arrived at Ffestiniog the scenery the whole way being exquisite we went through the vale of Ffestiniog. When we got to the station we walked to the Pengwern Arms a very grand hotel where we found everything to our comfort. The next morning there being no English Service under 3 miles from here we drove with some other people to church. In the afternoon we sat upon a high mound outside the churchyard (which is just near the Hotel) till it got cool. It was such a glorious day. In the evening Annie & I went a most lovely walk leaving Aunt Emma to listen to a Welsh service (which she did not understand) the place was so lovely it consisted of a wood through which rushed a torrent . . . In the afternoon [2 days later] Aunt Emma, Annie & I walked to the same place as we did on Sunday only by another route, we met several large dogs on the way (it is the custom of the Welsh to leave their cottages in charge of large dogs) we were rather frightened. . . . . . . . . . . . . The Welsh stare very much at one each time you pass they stand still and stare at last I have got used to it but it did seem peculiar at first also it appeared strange to me at first not to understand a word the people say and not be able to make them understand you it is rather awkward when you are walking and want to know the way I tried to learn the sentence "Which way does this road lead" in Welsh but it was no good as I could not make them comprehend me perhaps I spoke too fast.

*67* Diary of Isabel Adderley, 1868. Derbyshire Record Office, D2375M/ 180/20 (**107**)

*68* The Vale of Festiniog, by J H Grimm, 1781. Dyfed Archives Service, Castell Gorfod Colln, 313

# Scotland

*Over one hundred and fifty diaries, a quarter of the total and including the earliest, that of Christopher Lowther in 1629, feature visits to Scotland. Until the mid-nineteenth century, Edinburgh, Glasgow, the Lowlands and central region absorbed the interest of most travellers, among them many perceptive observers of Scottish agriculture, industries, trade, commerce and culture. Thereafter, new road, rail and ferry communications made touring in the Highlands and Isles possible for the ordinary holidaymaker, as well as popular for the tourist with more time.*

## Edinburgh in 1629

Now havinge passed through the courtes we will enter the towne in which there is but one street of note called the high street beginninge at the Castle & goinge downe to the Neitherbowe wch. is one of the barres or gates of the citty; & streighte on to the Abbe which is the kinges pallace but the streete from the Nether bowe to the Abbey is called the Cannagate; the one side of wch. is a liberty of it selfe the other side belonginge to Edinburgh; as Howburne one side to London the other to Westminster they have a fine Towbeoth & prison in it, this streete & the high street are but one street called by strangers; the next streete is Cowegate within the city as long as either of them but narrower; the reste but winds & closes; some 2 yardes broad. The Abbey is a very statly peece of worke, uniforme, & a dainty nete chappell in it; with a paire of organes in it & none els in the citty they being puritanes; there be fine prisons of a great height & fine hewne stone buildings; there be 5 Churches of which Sent Giles [is] the Chefe because of the stately steeple; . .

69  Diary of Christopher Lowther, 1629.   Cumbria Record Office, Carlisle, D/Lons/L2/4  (**91**)

## Edinburgh and Glasgow, 1760

The streets in this City are very narrow Except the Cannongate or high street the lanes they call Wynds & the Allys Closses. The Highth of the houses occasions great inconveniences as they must be inhabited by sevll familys & we were advised to keep house in the Evening as a Beastly Custom reigns here of Emptying all their Stink pots by hand out of the Window at night wch the Scavengers clean away early in the morning but I cannot say but this Custom together with that of the Women walking in the dirty streets all day without shoes or stockings together with the reall natural delight wch the Scotch people seem to take in nastiness renders an unwholsome Damd stench throughout the City all day . . . . . .
. . . from Dunbarton to Glasgow was a very pleasant and a fine Corn Country all the way by the side of the River Clyde. Glasgow is situated upon the river Clyde about 15m from the sea and is by much the best town in all respects in Scotland. There are 3 principal Streets in it. The Town carries on a great deal of foreign trade and there are a great many such Merchants live and it is one of the neatest built Town I ever saw in my life. There are 8 steples and a good University.

70  Diary of George Thornhill, 1760.   Cambridgeshire Record Office, Huntington,   148/5/274  (**48**)

## Visit to the Carron Ironworks, 1794

After Staying over Monday & Monday night (18 November) at Edinburgh we set out on Tuesday in a heavy Rain for Linlithgow to a Second Breakfast, but before we got half-way we found ourselves wet through and therefore

Stopt at Kirkleaton and got Dryed & got Breakfast & set of for Lithgow & before we reached it we were wet thro' a second time, here we got dry again, and set off for the Carron Works, which place we reached dry, after putting up our horses at a little pulic (sic) house we walked Cross the Bridge to the Works, here we met with the porter who carried us from one place to another so fast that we got no time to survey the different parts with that exactness necessary for such a wonderful manufacture, all produced from Stone, out of which Iron is extracted by Melting. At first he conducted us thro' a great many piles of Canon (sic) Balls, al 24lb then he shewed us Cannon Morters, of all sizes, fireplaces, Tea Kettles, pots, pans, fish kettles, grape shot, Chain shot, link Shot, Ban Shot, Grates, Heaters, Smothing (sic) Irons, & all the different productions of this wonderfull place, great Stoves, Spades, Shovels, Grapes, and everything produced from metal, the Great Bellows that were worked by Water, made such a Noise that I durst hardly Come near them, the sound Conveyed such an Idea of their bursting with excessive heat, that fear kept me from looking into them, then I saw thousands upon thousands of Cartloads of Ironstone brot. from so many different parts and immense Quantities of Lime Stones and Coals, & Sand to make their Molds of, there are On thousand men employed at this Place just now, we were Informed that trade was never known to be so brisk as at this time, owing to the Warr, calling for so many Guns, mortors, and Ball, Shot, &c. here is a very Great Canal on which I saw a Ship Rigged and Masted exactly like the Berwick Smacks, and I do suppose sails in the same manner, after saying all this about this wonderfull place, no man can do it sufficient justice, nor words can express the wonders contained in this Busy place.

71   Diary of Matthew Culley, 1794.   Northumberland Record Office, ZCU.1/4  **(454)**


## Description of Robert Owen's school at New Lanark, 1823

. . . set off to see Mr.Owen's school and the cotton spinning and the Falls of Clyde. Mr.Owen's school more interesting than I had expected – about 300 children. Saw them dancing, very pretty but great pity to put quadrille notions into their little heads; they also dance country dances and reels extremely well – queer dress, no shoes nor stockings, kind of thin petticoat up to their knees on both girls and boys . . . this made of white cotton material trimmed with blue or red so that they look just like opera dancers. Saw them also at a geographical lesson in some respects a good plan but one which makes as it appeared to me just the few who are anxious to learn quickly, but leaves the others ignorant. There was a great map unnamed the country on it. He the master pointed to it and asked the class all at once what it was – 2 or 3 always answered correctly, the others might be looking about the room but bawled out in concert. However 3 little girls between six and 7 answered well and seemed to have a clear idea of what they were about. Pictures of different branches of learning such as natural history, botany, a little anatomy, conchology, chronology etc were nicely drawn and hung up around the room. it is said they learn quickly a very neat and tolerably free running hand . . . Scripture read 2 in a week, Sabbath School commenced by prayer but Mr.Owen *does not like compulsion* so few come. When 10 years old they are taken into the cotton factory if they like but not till then.

72 Diary of Sarah Brinkley, August–September 1823. Clwyd Record Office, DD/PR/134 (**62**)

73 Dancing class in Robert Owen's school at New Lanark, 1825. Engraving by G. Hunt

## Queen Victoria at Braemar, 1869

11th (June), 6th day. As the wind and weather are not satisfactory, we have determined to wait for a change: so in order to employ the time profitably we took the Railway at 11 a.m. and arrived at Ballater about 2.30 p.m. Thence (after dining at the Invercauld Arms) we took a brace of Carriages: Katharine and myself and Jane in one; and Edwd B. and A. P. Mounsey, James Edward Backhouse and our yacht Captain, Caws, – in the other. Saw Balmoral Castle (where the Queen is now residing) and also Abergeldie Castle belonging to the Prince of Wales. Our nephews stopped to Photograph them: while my Wife and I went to visit the falls of Garrawalt. The view from the bridge above them was beautiful, the Cairn Gorum mountains with snow on them. The chief interest however was in the huge Scotch Firs in the park through which the road led to the falls: tho' the falls are small and pretty. Arrived at the Invercauld Arms at Castleton of Braemar about 6.45 p.m. It is very much warmer here than at Aberdeen. The handsome mountain Lochnagar, had a good deal of snow on it.

I had written so far when Queen Victoria in a black hat with a white feather drove past at a great rate making the dust fly: in a shabbyish carriage and pair. She had a huge "prog" basket behind.

12/6 mo. The Queen has again been here, and stopped about 5 p.m. for some time in her carriage in front of the Hotel. We had a good view of her. This time, Princess Beatrice sat next the Queen and had on a Glengarry. The Duchess dowager of Athole sat opposite the Queen & Flora McDonald next to her. Prince Leopold was on the box, along with the celebrated John Brown. We find that the great basket which fits behind, is full of wood & provisions as we supposed: as the Queen lights a fire (or has one lighted), and takes tea in the course of her excursions at some romantic spot as she may choose. She again drove past on her return about 7 p.m.

74    Diary of Edward Backhouse, with sketch of Queen Victoria and party, 1869.    Durham Record Office,    D/Wa 1/4/7    **(141)**

## A day at Chisholm Pass and Loch Beneveian in the Affric Mountains, September 1871

On to the Chisholm Pass occupying one of the three principal glens among the Affrich Mountains. The view the whole way was just as rich and glowing with beauty, as the landscape on first dipping into the valley appeared. The day improved in beauty if that was possible and by two o'clock the Daddy's friends' house was reached and there the excellent man gave our hungry wayfarers their lunch.

The house was a tiny shooting box, but with the most ingenious spare bed rooms that have ever been devised. Batchelors' bedrooms built on the enlarged & improved Kennel plan!

Very little time was given to luncheon. The Misses Dove, the gentle nieces of the host, walked part of the way towards the pass with the Artist and Mary and then sent them up the Pass in their own carriage with instructions to drive up to a summer loghouse they had at the head of the Pass, order tea there and row on the Loch named Beneveian so as to see the mountains from the water.

Entrance to Chisholme Pass

Loch Beneveian — at
Head of Chisholme Pass.

All this they did and drove back again about six in the evening after such a sight of gorgeous, wondrous beauty as they had never witnessed before – it cannot be described.

Miles and miles of beautiful gentle waving birch forests with dark tender greens of scotch firs intermingling here and there – blue grey, silver and gold mountains in the distance, the nearer ones clothed with this wondrous forest too. And the foot of the mountains dropping down in its many coloured leafy garb, to a river foaming white and amber, brown, purple, coloured waters – with the sheer naked rock peeping out between the birches, or through the water, just here and just there, where one would wish it to be. But the miles of forest trees were what perhaps impressed English eyes most – and that drive, that day's wonderful exquisite views laid fair to be treasures as one of their most lovely memories by the Lawyer, the Artist and Mary.

75   Diary and sketches by Laura Elizabeth Palmer, 1871.   Hampshire Record Office,   9M68/63   (**271**)

76   Braemar Castle, 1869. Watercolour by Edward Backhouse.   Durham Record Office,   D/Wa 12/4/7   (**141**)

# Visiting Country Houses

*Unexpectedly, the diaries, even from the eighteenth century, reveal a popular interest in seeing over the mansions of noblemen and gentry, a readiness of owners to show visitors around, regular opening hours, with a tour by the housekeeper, and at Kedleston in 1816 even a guide book, while the parks and grounds seem similarly to have been open for leisurely recreation. The diarists show an appreciation of the paintings, art treasures and architecture of houses, reflecting their taste and education.*

# Powis Castle and countryside, 1755

From thence we travelled with infinite pleasure through the most pleasing country my eye ever beheld or my imagination can present, to Powis Castle, part of which was burnt down about 30 years ago, but there still remains a great house situated so finely, so nobly, that were I in the place of Lord Powis, I should forsake Okeley park with all its beauties, and fix my seat there, as the most eligible in every respect. About £3000 laid out upon it would make it the most august in the Kingdom. It stands on the side of a very high hill; below is a vale of incomparable beauty with the Severn winding through it. The opposite side is beautifully cultivated half way up and green to the very top except one or two hills, which are rocky and grotesque, shapes that give a variety and spirit to the prospect. Above the Castle is a long ridge of hills finely shaded, part of which is the Park, and higher still is a terress up to which you are led through very fine lawns and from whence you have a view that exceeds all description . . . The inclosures are shaded in with very fine hedgrows, there is a lovely mixture of cornfield and meadows, though more of the latter; the vales and bottoms are large and the mountains that rise like a rampart all around add a magnificence and grandeur to the scene without giving you any horrid or dreadful ideas.

*77*   Diary of Sir George Lyttelton, 5th Bt, 1st Lord Lyttelton, 1755.   Clwyd Record Office,   D/E/1209   **(52)**

*78*   Powis Castle, from *The Beauties of England and Wales*, by J Evans, Vol XVII, Part 1, 1812.

## Kedleston Hall, 'the most magnificent in this country', 1771

Ld Scarsdales house at Keddlestone is the most magnificent in this country both in architecture and in furniture. You enter into a hall of an oblong form, the size of which is 60 by 30 ft., and 40 high. It is lighted by the means of 3 oval skylights. on either side is a row of Corinthian pillars of alabaster, to the number of 20 in all. This leads to a saloon that is a regular circle of 42ft diameter, and 44.6 inches high.

The Principal drawing room is 44 × 28 and 28 high. The doors are in general mahogany, elegantly carved – the chimney pieces of alabaster or diff. marble of the country with the curious pieces of petrifications – stone called blue jack – inlaid. The cases to the windows are sometimes of marble or alabaster.

The ceilings are painted by Moreland. The window frames on the outside are gilt in the same manner as at Chatsworth. Immediately in front of the house is a new bridge of a handsome construction, which wants however great part of its effect, as it has not yet any water flowing under it.

*79* Diary of Luttrell Wynne, 1771. Cornwall Record Office, PH 464 **(68)**

*80* Kedleston, by Luttrell Wynne, 1771. Cornwall Record Office, PD 439 **(70)**

## A visit to Kedleston in 1816

(King's Head, Derby). Friday, 9th August. Breakfast, marketing and sundry consultations as to the route we should pursue occupied the first part of the morning, but nine o'clock found us in the carriage and bound for Kedleston, the seat of Lord Scarsdale. We reached it before ten and at the Lodge learned to our dismay the house was not shewn till 11. What could be done? It was judged best to put a good face on the matter & proceed towards the mansion. Arrived there, we informed them of our mistake and My Lord who saw us from the window politely ordered we might not be kept waiting. On entering the Hall, we were each presented with a book containing an account of all we were to see, the subjects of the pictures and names of the painters: a good plan as it saves many questions and probably gives more accurate information.

*81*   Diary of Mary Anne Hibbert, 1816.   Gloucestershire Record Office, D1799/F320  **(221)**

## Warwick Castle, 1771

*83*   Warwick Castle, 1771.   Sketchbook of Luttrell Wynne.   Cornwall Record Office,   DD.PD 439  **(70)**

In the evening I arrived at Warwick. The principal object of a Traveller's curiosity in this Town is the Castle, the seat of the Earl of Warwick. The noble elevated situation of this fine piece of antiquity, its park abounding with plantations & diversity of grounds immediately adjacent to it (lay'd out in the modern taste) & the windings of the River below render it altogether a scene as noble & pleasing as any in the Kingdom of the same sort. Nothing can be more venerable & awfull than the first court you enter, surrounded with antique Towers, turrets & battlements. The range of state rooms are grand, & furnished in a taste suitable to the structure of which they are part. Indeed, it may be observed, to the honour of its owner, that the whole is kept in a state of repair conformable to the original design of it. The best view of this Castle, its environs, & the Town is from the Lodge in the Park . .

*82* Diary of Luttrell Wynne, 1771. Cornwall Record Office, DD.PD 464 (**68**)

## Stansted Hall, 1809

Drove to Stansted Mount Fitchet Castle, a very large ancient house; it appears a great deal to see outside but found nothing within except two Rooms, one Cedar, and the other Brown Oak, – both handsomely carved and handsome Chimney pieces. Some fine Tapestry, a large Hall and grand Staircase richly carved, would have done honour to Burghley: some old China and a few good pictures bought at the Duke of Bedford's Sale.

*84* Diary of Millicent Bant, 1809. Essex Record Office, D/Fr F4 (**184**)

*85* Stansted Hall, c.1809, from *Excursions in Essex*, Vol. II.

# How the Other Half Lives

*Tourists then as now could not travel far without seeing
something of the harsh working and living conditions of the
mass of the labouring poor. But, with exceptions, diarists who
almost incidentally record clear evidence of hardship and
inequality refrain from social comment, though it seems
inconceivable that they could be unaffected by obvious distress.*

## Hiring day at Rhuddlan, 1750

Sunday the 20th. Stay'd at Redland, where I went to Church; the Service is in both Welch, and English; the Prayers were read in Welch, & the Psalms & Chapters in English & then the Sermon was Preach'd in Welch; They also sung a Psalm, wch. is sometimes in English, & sometimes in Welch . . They have an odd Custome Here, . . . wch. is, the manner of Hiring their Husbandry people. After Church is over in the Morning, all the Farmers & People that want to Hire Servants meet in the Middle of the Parish, (or sometimes if the Church yard is a large one they meet there, but its generally in the Broadest part in the parish, that will contain a number of People) where all the Men, & Women that come to be Hired stand, with their Rakes, & Rip hookes, and other Husbandry impliments in their Hands; its a vast Crowd of People, for they come both to Hire & be Hired from all the Villages & Towns round about, & lookes like a Fair, & after having each made the best bargain they can (& some Farmers Hire thirty People some times, the Man of the House where we were Hired five & Twenty) they carry 'em, each Man the servants he has Hired to the Ale House, to treat 'em with Ale, and after they have all Drank, they generally all the young Men, & Maids, take a Dance, & if they have any money themselves to continue this Entertainment, it lasts quite till the Evening, & in the place where they are Hired there is people that set & sell Cakes, & Fruit, so that all together it is quite an Odd Sight upon a Sunday, to people that are not used to it, & in the House where we were the Hearing the Fidle playing & the People some Danceing & some Singing made one hardly believe it was Sunday, but at other times they are very regular, & constant, in going to church.

*86*  Diary of William Mildmay, 1750.  Essex Record Office,  C/DMy
15 M 50/1325  **(180)**


## 'A Detestable piece of Slavery': women carrying coal, 1771

Thursday, 21st (November 1771). A Remarkable fine Morning. I Breakfasted at Blackshields, Mr Fairbarns, a very good House, I must remark again what a Fertile Shoot of Land is from Edenbro. on this side Dalkeith, where is one of those Coalpitts, from which the Coals are brought up upon Womens Shoulders, in a kind of basket slung over their heads by a rope. What a Detestable piece of Slavery is this. I should not have thought that such a piece of Barbarity could at this time have Existed, If I had not been an Eye Wittness of it. The Women who do this disagreeable Jobb are called Bearers, & they may add Mourners too, I think, for it must be a Sorrowfull task.

*87*  Diary of George Culley, 1771.  Northumberland Record Office,
ZCU.1/3  **(452)**

*87a*  Woman carrying coal, East of Scotland, 1841.  *Children's Employment Commission Report*, 1841

## Poor House, Newport, Isle of Wight, 1776

Friday, Septr. 6th. set out at Seven in the Morning for Cowes, soon after leaving Newport on the Right we saw a large brick building, lately erected for the humane purpose of maintaining their poor, we were told it contain'd five hundred at present . . . .

*88*  Anonymous diary, 1776.   Isle of Wight Record Office,   81/98   (**326**)


## A Highland farm house, 1807

Went into an Highland farm House, which consisted of three holes, in the first was a Fire in the middle of the ground without any aperture for the escape of the smoke, in the second was the Bed and in the third was a Cow and Calf, and all manner of Rubbish. For this Hovel, with a small Potatoe Garden, and feed on the Mountain for one Cow, these poor Creatures pay £7 a year and call it a large farm House. Arrived at Inverrary a tolerable Inn.

*89*  Diary of Millicent Bant, 1807.   Essex Record Office,   D/DFr F2   (**183**)


## 'Wretched habitations', near Bala, North Wales, 1808

From a country fertile and romantic in the extreme, we now entered upon a wild desolate tract, barren of wood and miserably cultivated, rendered more dreary likewise by the sorry appearance of a few hovels, scattered at solitary distances over this immense waste. The architecture of these wretched habitations is truly simple. Built of a slaty stone, slovenly put together with a mere handful of cement, and thatched with turf, they contain, in general, no more than one room, lighted by a small window, for the accommodation of a whole family. The fire place consists of a large flag fixed in one corner of the room, having an aperture in the roof above it which serves as a chimney. Turf is their only fuel.

*90*  Anonymous diary, 1808.   Clwyd Record Office,   DD/DM/228/ 78   (**60**)


## 'Where darkness and eternal horror reign': visit to a Staffordshire Ironworks, 1825

Thursday, July 21st (1825). We proceeded on our journey to Snelstone Ironworks where we got out to see the different processes the ore undergoes & brought away some specimens. Some hundreds of men are employed here, some but slightly clothed & with plates over their legs & feet to protect them from the immense fires & there were several children apparently not more than ten or twelve years old, rolling out red hot Bars of Iron weighing forty pounds. The thick black smoke that ascended on all sides from the numerous coalpits & the swarthy appearance of the half dressed inhabitants, almost led one to imagine we were paying a visit to the lower regions where "darkness & eternal horror reign".

91   Diary of Eliza Spurrett, 1825.   Leicestershire Record Office,   7D54/2/1
     (**372**)


## Saturday shoppers in Birmingham, 1834

This being the last evening of the week many of the neighbouring towns as well as the suburbs of Birmingham had poured forth their numbers to purchase the necessaries which are used on the Sundays and which calls forth greater varieties than on any other day on account of the wages being received. I had the opportunity of contrasting the style of the population of Birmingham with London and as far as such a comparison can be made, deducting external appearance, I should almost be inclined to say that the former has a larger proportion of happy faces although in rougher habiliments. They crowded as thick as the population in St. Giles and almost as dirty; but all seemed joy and the coming holiday hailed by all with pleasure.

92   Diary of William Graeme Tomkins, CE, 1834.   Clwyd Record
     Office,   DD/DM/365/1   (**64**)

# The Industrial Revolution

*To reach their destinations, be they distant hills or health-giving waters, tourists had to travel slowly in stages along well-worn highways through busy manufacturing towns and industrial landscapes. Some hurried on; others paused to note trades and occupations, investigate local manufactures, see notable engineering feats. Travellers of enquiring minds were shown over factories, had processes explained to them, examined new machinery. As most diaries date between 1750 and 1850, they provide a fruitful commentary on the transformation of British industry and agriculture during this century.*

## Draining coal pits by water power, 1676

From Haddington we went on that morning first to Musselburgh where is a very fair old house of ye Earle of Tweedales just by Musselborough Town which is a large Town scituate neare the city and not far from whence are great Coalpitts and saltpans belonging to ye now Duke of Lauderdaile. Wee staid to see both and did very much admire the invention they had of Drayning the Coalpitts where the Water draws up the Water for above 50 fathoms by Turning a wheele which letts down Bucketts by a chaine into the water as it were into a great deep well and draws them up again and after they come up full as they Turne to go downe again with the Bottomes uppermost they empty themselves into a Trough and so convey away the Water, there are 32 of these Bucketts fastened to a chaine and 2 severall chaines and the Bucketts are abt 10 foot distance from one another and hold abt as much as 2 ordinary Pales. but one chaine of Bucketts workes att one time and when the water is scarce to turne the Wheele they have on the Top of it a place to do it by horses.

*93* Diary of John Conyers, 1676.  Essex Record Office,  D/DW Z6/1 (**178**)

## Newcastle coal roads, 1760

*95* Horse drawn coal waggons on a Tyneside waggon-way leading to a coal staith for off-loading into keels, 1787.

All the Country between Durham and Newcastle is supposed to Contain Coal, almost every where we continually met along these roads the particular sort of cart they make use of to carry these coals to the Ryver Tyne, from whence they Carry them Seven Miles in Keels or Lighters to Sheals (Shields) to put them on Shipboard. There are a vast Quantity of Coal roads every where within ten miles of Newcastle & the wheels of the Carts wch are made of Iron and very low, run upon Wood – the friction is so

small that the Cartsfull containing 3 tun are drawn from the pitts twice a day by one horse 7m & upon the least descent they go a great pace without horses, so that a lean small horse goes 28m per day & what is remarkable the Cart Empty is more difficult for the horse to draw than when full.

*94*    Diary of George Thornhill, 1760.    Cambridgeshire Record Office, Huntingdon,    148/5/274    (**48**)

## Lord Bridgewater's canal over the River Irwell, 22 June 1771

But at BARTON, about two Miles from Worsley, was an Obstacle that would have stopped the Progress of less skilful, or less spirited Undertakers. for here a deep Valley, a navigable River and two public Roads thwarted the Course of the Navigation, but all this was subdued. the Valley, almost a Furlong in Breadth, was filled up with Earth; a noble Bridge of 3 Arches (the largest of which is 63 Feet wide) was thrown over the River: and every Thing being made level, the Canal carried over the whole. the Canal here is 6 Yards over; with a Path on each side of it half as broad.

This is a most capital scene. to see Ships, sailing, as it were in the Air, 50 Yards above a navigable River, cannot fail of striking the Spectator with the most pleasing Astonishment.

But here was also a public Road running on each side of the River. to have carried these over the Canal by Bridges (as had been practised in level Parts) would here have been a prodigious Expence, as they must have been of so great a length: they are therefore conducted, with an inconsiderable Descent and Ascent, through Arches, beneath it. –

*96*    Diary of Rev Sir John Cullum, 1771.    Suffolk Record Office, E2/44/1 (**538**)

*97*    'View of part of the Duke of Bridgewater's Navigation cross the Irwell', c.1771. Diary of Rev Sir John Cullum, 1771.    Suffolk Record Office,    E2/44/1 (**538**)

# The salt trade of Northwich, 1771

Northwich is a small neat built commercial town 7 m distant (from Knutsford). Salt is so considerable an article of trade in this place as to bring in 100,000£ yearly to ye government by ye duties on it. The Pits from whence it comes are well worth seeing, where it is hewn out of ye solid rock of which it is part. They are about 60 yards deep, down which you are to descend in a bucket, abᵗ half way is a landing place just above which ye Briny water collects itself in a sort of well.

By ye next shaft you descend imediately into ye pit. It is curious to observe ye manner in which ye works are prevented from falling in, of which no kind of danger appears from ye security given them by 4 massy pillars of this salt left at each opening which run throughout ye whole at 8 yards asunder, the height of which and ye extent of ye pits give a great grandeur to ye work. The salt in some places was entirely pure but in general it is obliged to be melted, which however is done without ye assistance of fire to evaporate ye watery part. This operation is done chiefly at Liverpool (but little being done here) to which there is a navigable cut from hence. Great quantitys are shipped from hence to other parts of ye Kingdom.

*98*   Diary of Luttrell Wynne, 1771.   Cornwall Record Office,   PD 465   (**69**)

*99*   Northwich Old Bridge, c.1830.   Cheshire Record Office, SF:Northwich

# The process of silver plating observed at Sheffield, 27 July 1799

The Silver Plating Manufactory which we saw was Messrs. Goodman & Co's. We saw the whole process, which is

1st. The ingots of copper are fastened to those of silver with Wire, & a little Borax disolved in water insinuated into the joining. These are then put in the oven & the heat unites them.

2nd. They are rolled out, by a Hand Mill

3rd. They are formed according to the shape wanted. If for round candlesticks, The bottom is stamped whole, & the neck in three pieces which when united makes it compleat. If oval, generally one half (cut perpendicularly) is stamped at once. Tea Pots & Urns are beat out by much time & trouble, from a flat surface. The dies are made of Steel & cut out by hand, & the corresponding part, which is to face the plating to the shape, is lead pound into the die, & fastened to the weight of the *Stamp* (or Press) by holes in the weight & the lead being soft, presses into the holes when the weight falls.

5th. The superflous parts are then cut off &

6thly. They are soldered together, if but a small place with silver & brass (called Hard Solder), if a large space, with Lead & Tin (called soft Solder). The former is a hard substance, & is applied in small slips cut out according to the size & shape wanted. It is melted by a Blow Pipe & Lamp. The latter is applied in the common way by a hot Iron with rosin. The seams or joinings are then burnished & the whole is finished up. For the purpose of engraving they have a method of making the Silver plating thicker in one part then another.

*100* Diary of Thomas Philip, 3rd Lord Grantham, 1799. Bedfordshire Record Office, L31/114/3 (**17**)

# A black and gloomy impression of Sheffield, 1823

Approaching Rotherham the county assumed a gloomy dark appearance, the very trees, roads, hedges are black. We passed through it and changed horses at Sheffield – in fact it is all one and the same. The road is pavé and thickly populated. To render the scene more charming a man hanging in a gallows by it seem'd quite in character. All was black and gloom, the day too was in keeping not a gleam of sun nor rain nor wind; all this dark black smoaky atmosphere was the creation of a thousand steam ingines and factories, iron founderies and general business. We visited at Sheffield Messrs Rodgers steel manufactory the first in the world and made a few purchases also Messrs Gainsfords Plate workers in Eyre Street where we saw the mode of making plated articles. We were, not withstanding the temptation offered us of seeing more of this emporium of cutlery, anxious and nothing loth to get far from the place.

*101* Diary of E J Esdaile, 1823. Somerset Record Office, DD/ES Box 17 (**510**)

# A machine for spinning cotton inspected at Manchester, 23 July 1799

We went next to (a) large Factory for spinning cotton. The Carding is done by machinery & the Cotton is then passed thro a narrow space which presses it clous together: four of these threads are then passed thro & pressed together, & after that it receives a slight twist by being passed thro a still narrower space & dropped into a tin cannister which is turned round quick & by that means slightly twists the thread: this is afterwards wound on spindles & twisted harder by a sort of Jenny. The final operation is putting 2 or more of these threads together & twisting them by the Jenny, the chief perfection of which is the contrivance for permitting only a certain length of the coarse thread to pass thro the rollers at once, which length is extended & twisted harder afterwards till at last the Machine stops of itself. The man who attends, pushes it back & by that means winds the Cotton spun on the spindle. He then puts the Wheels *in gear* & the Machine goes on. The different parts of the Machine are stopt separately by putting those parts out *of gear* (i.e. throwing the cogs of the wheels asunder) which is effected by a Peg in an arm of a Wheel which presses down a Lever once in a revolution & by that means looses a catch & the Wheel falls out of Gear by its own weight. The Machine is stopt by the same sort of contrivance. When the thread is wound up for sale, they wind it in *Lays*, each 140 yards, 7 lays to a Hank, & of the finest Cotton 22 Hanks to a lb, that is 215, 600 yards, or 122½ miles. . . . . .

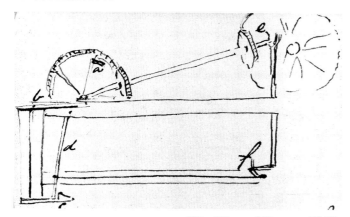

a. the peg which presses upon & lifts up the Lever (b) which is connected with the latch (c). When the bar (d) is let go by (c) being depressed the wheel (e) falls out of gear, & when (d) is replaced it pulls the elbow (f) & again puts (e) in gear.

*102*    Diary of Thomas Philip, 3rd Lord Grantham, 1799.    Bedfordshire Record Office,   L31/114/3   **(17)**

## Tour of Portsmouth Dockyards, 1811

After driving (I thought it) a long way through very narrow, dirty streets, very much like some of Wapping, we found the Royal Oak Inn (where we had been recommended) and putting in our horses etc went directly (about 20 mi. past 11) to the gates of the dock-yard, where we were told it was too late for admittance, but after a little parley, learnt a gentleman with his family were coming in about 2 hours, when *perhaps* we might get in with them – in the interim we got a boatman to take us about the harbour. . . . . .

Got back just as the workmen (about 3,000) were returning from dinner; again found some difficulty in gaining admittance, but after putting down our names, and places of residence, in a large book we hurry'd forward to join a party who had just entered, were first shown some ships in the dry docks, undergoing repairs etc. and saw two, or three, on the stocks a-building, next went to the house were [sic] the copper is melted, and afterwards rolled into plates, for covering the ships bottoms, the rolling of the copper after casting is performed by a steam engine of 40 horse-power, it was a very curious process, but the most so of any is the making of Blocks (what we should call pullys) which are used about the rigging, it is all performed by means of a steam-engine (of 30 horse power) sawing, turning, boring etc. in a very expeditious manner, it was all together a very entertaining sight – we next arrived at the Smith's work shop where the large anchors, and all the other iron work wanted about a ship is made, it is a very long, lofty building with a row of large furnaces, on each side, it was a dismal black looking place reminding one of the fabulous accounts of old Vulcan and his forges – we were not permitted to enter the rope walk (as no strangers are) so could not see much of that work only by looking in at the door, the men apper'd to work harder at it than at any of the other processes.

*103*   Diary of William Wilshere, 1811.   Hertfordshire Record Office, 61175   (**319**)


## Worcester Porcelain Factory, 1814

The view of Worcester on the road from Malvern is by far the best you have of the city in any situation and is very striking. Inn, the Hop pole, very good. The town is a remarkably nice looking town, handsome, very clean & the streets wide & well paved, the houses good & the shops the same. It is famed for the manufactory of porcelain, which is made of flint burnt & other materials pound together & then burnt again. It is then made into a clay and either formed by the hands into plates, cups & saucers, coffee cups, &c., or made by the use of molds into teapots, urns or any fancy pieces. They are then, when dry, put into a furnace & heated to a certain degree when they are passed thro a mixture of the consistency of rich (?) paste, which causes a coat of glazing. It is made chiefly of white lead & vinegar is mixed with it. This part of the business appears to be the most hurtful, and the boys employed in it looked pale & sickly. When finished here, the pieces are taken to the painting room. Those employed in this branch must be able to bear great heat as the windows never can be open for fear of the dust flying into the room & fixing on the colours before they are dry. They are obliged to have a very strong light, & all have shades as without them their sight, it is said, would be much injured. After the painting is done, they are then burnished. This is done by women who use for the purpose of burnishing a piece of bloodstone & by rubbing hard & for a time together produce this last finish on the china. . . . . All the ornamental parts of the China are made by hand & then fixed on to the piece by some of the mixture of which the clay is composed when it is in a liquid state.

*104* Diary of Sir Mathew White Ridley Bt, 1814.   Northumberland Record Office,   ZRI.31/3/8   **(459)**

*105* Royal China Manufactory of Messrs Flight and Barr, Worcester, 1795.   Hereford & Worcester Record Office

## Birmingham in 1819

*Birmingham* good view of the extent of the Town from the Country Road. Whip manufactory. covering the stick with the plat done in ¾ of an hour. formerly took 4 boys 4 days. Stick made of Lance wood some covered with brass wire for Bueno Ayres. Chief mart S. America. the manufacturer exports his own whips. at first refused admittance, fear of rival manufactorers from the Continent. Mr. Thomason's Warwick Vase nearly complete, all the parts put together. Vases in imitation of China in the same state as last year.

from Birmingham to *Wolverhampton* one continued street. Country around an amphitheatre of blazing furnaces.

*106*   Diary of Lady Philadelphia Cotton, 1819.   Cambridgeshire Record Office,   588/F48   **(47)**


## 'Made in Birmingham', 1834

We set out after our breakfast for Mr. Thomason's show rooms . . . we saw young Mr. Thomason and . . . when we had looked over the show rooms which are very extensive, he told us that if we could return in an hour we should have the workshops open to our inspection . . . We returned to Mr T. at ½ past 11 and were admitted over the works . . . The mysteries here exhibited to our admiring and enquiring gaze (to enumerate shortly) consisted of 1stly button making and burnishing, making the shanks and ornamenting it, the latter two of which are done by machines exceedingly curious and complicated – 2nd the burnishing of silver plate, making silver knives and handles, embossing plate, striking medals (which I performed in Queens metal) lapidary work and finally the modelling in wax for casting silver and bronze.

*107*   Diary of William Graeme Tomkins, 1834.   Clwyd Record Office, DD/DM/365/1   **(64)**

# Incidents on the Way

*As well as being compulsive scribblers, many diarists were also of sharp observation and ready wit. Many incidents on the way are recorded. Some were undoubtedly of a serious nature at the time, such as a carriage breakdown, an encounter with a footpad, a violent storm leading to a thorough wetting; others were obviously trivial, like a spoilt luncheon or a playful exchange with Welsh children. An incident being over and done with, its humorous side often becomes apparent, and the cheerfulness which pervades the retelling in diary entries endears one to the writer.*

## Russian sailors at Leith, 1794

On the sunday Evening (17 November) after Tea we took a walk down to Lieth (sic) to see the Russian Squadron of 11 Ships, five of them are line of Battle Ships, two of them 74 Gun Ships, the rest frigates, which ships are lying in Leath (sic) Roads, in our going down we saw a great many Russians coming and going too and from the town, some drunk, some sober, chatteringand jabbering like as many Monkies in the Russian language. They are in General a Stout people not handsome rather sallow Complection, that is perhaps owing to being on board the Ships for Sailors in general are sallow faced. On Monday they were going about the Streats selling and exchanging their money and Some had Coarse Cloth, Boots, Shoes, Slippers, &c. to sell or exchangefor English money or goods – while I was standing in my friend Mr. Millers Shop there was one Russian Came in seemingly a man of some Rank by his Dress, & he wanted to buy some poket handkerchiefs, he pulled one out of his poket, signifying he wanted something of that kind, on being shewed some, he gave us to understand that the Square was not large enough, by drawing 2 lines with his fingers on the Counter, & then Crossing them again, but he could not be pleased with any, then he loosed his Waiscoat & pulled out his neckcloth, meaning that he wanted something like that, and after a great deal to do in examining & asking the price of them (he could speak some English) he bought one at 2s. 6d., and when he came to pay the money he did it in Russ Money, Shewing us many different Coins of very Coarse Silver and one of Gold, in value about 12 Shillings, but he Called it a Guinea, but my friend would take none of his Coin, till he paid it with 2 Engh. Shillings, & two pieces in value about 6d., and he went away in a very bad humour, & we thot. he was swearing at us, because we would not take his Russian money, & he did not wish to part with his English Shillings – his Dress was very much like the English, he had on a Blue wide Coat, made Quite in the English fashion, with large Steel Carved Buttons, on dark Brown (Clowded with Green) Strait Coat, double Breasted in the late fashion, with Coverd large buttons, a flowered green Satten Waist Coat, Single Breasted and worsted Breaches, with Cotton Stockings, Shoes, & fashionable Buckles, lace tied, which they all have from the high to the lowest Ranks, & the old to the Young.

*108*   Diary of Matthew Culley, 1794.   Northumberland Record Office, ZCU.1/4   (**454**)


## 'Friends, go up higher'

Sunday, 11th August (1816). All up betimes, as we were not sufficiently pleased with our accommodations to wish to prolong the bliss by breakfasting at Buxton. The morning was blustering till about 10 o'clock when the wind subsided and a heavy rain came on. We breakfasted at Disley and found the provisions very tolerable, though we surmised they did not often see much genteel company from the pains they took to convince us that a party who came in *their own* carriage slept there the night before. The Church was near the Inn and we resolved to attend the service before we proceeded notwithstanding the rain. We muffled ourselves up in our Duffle Cloaks and mixed with the vulgar herd, but there was yet a something about us which marked the elevated sphere to which we belonged, for having seated ourselves in the first empty pew we saw, the Clergyman actually left the reading desk to say "Friends, go up higher". This honourable seat when we reached it proved a sort of cage in which we could neither hear nor see, but such is the ordinary tax of greatness . . . . . .

*109*  Diary of Mary Anne Hibbert, 1816.   Gloucestershire Record
       Office,   D1799/F320  **(221)**


## The luncheon basket, a poor traveller, 1816

Monday, 30th September (1816) (on the road to Knutsford). Nothing remarkable occurred till we had left Northwich when William's little inside began to want support, and he bent the whole of his nervous mind to the examination of the prog basket, when, oh woeful to relate, he found that, owing to this same basket having been an outside passenger without springs, the sandwiches, buns and gingerbreads were all jumbled into one indiscriminate paste and required a keen appetite to digest them. However, the case was urgent, the provision was demolished, and William and Sarah amused themselves by versifying our disaster . . . . .

*110*  Diary of Mary Anne Hibbert, 1816.   Gloucestershire Record
       Office,   D1799/F320  **(221)**


## Anxious moments crossing Morecambe Bay, 1804

Sept 13th. Nine o'clock resume our Route to Ulverston, over Lancaster sands (& never shall I forget it) the morning was dark & Gloomy – Sophia in the time of Breakfast entertained us with shocking accounts of the peril & danger of the attempt from intelligence she had learnt from the wife of the Postman whom she protested she gave up for lost whenever he left her – her Ladyship was not to be dismayed so set forward with the Caravan consisting of two stages a Cart 2 Horsemen. When we reached Hest Bank found the Tide too high – so alighted at the ferry House to await its going off – A young person passenger in one of the stages & encountered in the Garden had she informed me Crossed five & twenty times & only was in danger of drowning once, but confesed it was not in general conceivd to be safe – this gave us some alarm, but at last we enterd on the sands very Courageously – tho the wind blew the Clouds hung as it were in dread suspence over the Tremendous mountains – When we came to the first of seven fords we had to Cross – two was half a mile over (& this was one of those) rapid deep & wide – the singularity of the scene – the appearance of the Guide – the silence of every individual, broken only by the hoarse voice of the Guide Bawling We were too far to the right, or left, the Ocean, – Rocks, – flocks of sea Fowl, hovering over us, – the immense plain of sand & distance from Land, – joind to the hysteric screams of poor Sophia which now assaild our Ears (whose fears had been executed to the highest pitch before by the postmans wife) so worked upon our feelings that it is not easy to convey an idea of our strange situation, – When about midway we met 2 postchaise 2 Carts & one Horseman with a Chariot & attendants – this circumstance exhilirated our spirits wonderfully – and we proceeded with tolerable Composure to Cross Ulverston sands.

*111*   Diary of Millicent Bant, 1804.   Essex Record Office,   D/DFr F1   **(182)**

## Fellow passengers on a Highland voyage, 1832

After leaving Oban I happened to go on deck and was amusing myself for some time with studying the different characters on board. The first I had occasion to notice was a person talking French to Fletcher – a short thick man in a hat & coat more respectful than respectable who seemed on perfectly familiar terms with everyone and his own qualifications in particular. He claimed acquaintance with some of my family – talked of the nuns at Shepton Mallet – made a digression in favour of his friend Dr Coombes – gave the eulogism of Bishop Baines and concluded with his own history which I afterwards found he repeated to everyone that was unfortunate enough to come within the range of his elocution – in short he was a Frenchman.

Another character was a lady probably on the nameless side of forty with long dark eyebrows which came within a most [minute] distance of each other, deep sunk hazel eyes, a sharp smooth nose and chin and thin lips that appeared strained close to the teeth & each other by a frequent sharp application of the tongue within. My first introduction to her was seeing her with a bunch of grouse in her hand when we first came on board ordering about the vessel and scolding at the very top of her voice for the recovery of a carpet bag which belonged to her son though he assured her he had already seen it safe on board. She was travelling with her daughter, rather a pretty young lady of about 19 I shd. suppose, who seemed rather disposed to make her remarks on every one about, and her son a good natured henpecked youth of perhaps 18 who seemed to attend to the wants of his mother & sister rather for the sake of appearances than for any love of either of them.

*112*   Diary of Charles Weld, 1832.   Dorset Record Office,   D.16/F19   **(131)**

## St Mary's, Isles of Scilly, 1849

Went on deck about 7 o'clock as we were nearing the Scilly Isles. The coast is very bare and rocky and did not promise us much welcome. A pilot came on board and we sailed into the harbour of St. Mary's Island and anchored at ½ past 8 a.m. At 2 o'clock we went on shore to explore the island and walked nearly all over it. The principal town, Hugh Town, lookes comfortable and has some respectable houses in it, but there is a complete absence in this island of any thing like a tree. The heat was intense and we met with no shade in our walk which made it very much more fatiguing. The first town that was built in this island is still called Old Town and consists of a few small houses and a little church, of which there is now very little left and that is in a very neglected and wretched state. This church was a very good sized one but the present proprietor of this island pulled down almost the whole of it to build a large church in Hugh Town.

Church at St Mary's July 13th

In the evening we were alarmed by loud cries from a sloop a little way from us – as if someone was being murdered and they became louder and louder crying "murder, murder". In an instant the gig was lowered 25 men with Mr. Godden jumped in and pulled off to the sloop, found 2 men doing their best to kill the third and as they were all tipsy it is most likely they would have succeeded if help had not been at hand. The poor half killed wretch was taken on shore and the others fined. These two ruffians were afterwards obliged to continue their voyage without the other hand as he wisely declined having anything more to do with them.

*113* Diary of Elizabeth Mary Rolls on board *Esmeralda*, 1849. Sketch by J E W Rolls. Gwent Record Office, D.361 F/P.4.66, 70 **(257)**

## Storm at Torquay, 1852

Had a delightful sail back to Torquay and sent the visitors back to Torre Abbey much pleased with their day. Although at this time the weather was fine and we had no idea of a gale, at ½ past 12 a perfect tempest arose and we passed a most wretched night tossing and tumbling about – the rain coming down in torrents, wind whistling through the rigging and the vessel plunging against the anchor chain, John was up all night and passed a most anxious time the danger being of the chain giving way and of the vessel turning ashore. We had 60 fathoms of chain out and another anchor ready to let down – the Gipsy Queen, Fancy, Ballerina and Beatrice were our fellow sufferers and two of the yachts got under weigh with difficulty and went out to sea. The Camilla weathered the storm beautifully but the passengers in her were nevertheless particularly wretched and until we were tempted by the prospect of going ashore some of us would not attempt to get up – at 2 we left the vessel and a pretty tossing and wetting we got in the boats getting ashore, though the tempest was abating . . . . . .

**Afloat**

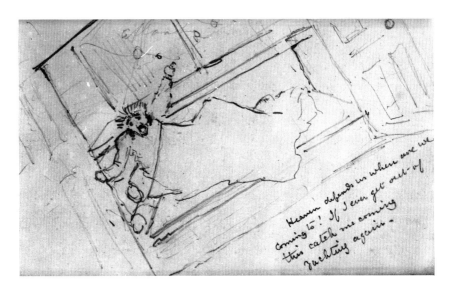

**Ashore**

No sooner were we safe in the hotel than the appetites of the ladies were restored and there was an immediate outcry for luncheon . . . . . . there were parties of yachtsmen to be seen all day in groups under the window talking over the gale and the perils to which they [had] been exposed and surmising what had become of the yachts that were missing – several uncomfortable reports having arisen as to the fate of some of the smaller ones. Red caps had been seen floating about also a portmanteau and it was said that 2 yachts and a merchantman had been seen to go down.

114   Diary of Elizabeth Mary Rolls on board *Camilla*, 1852.   Sketches by J E W Rolls.   Gwent Record Office,   D.361 F/P.4.65, 72   **(258)**

## 'An amusing encounter' with Welsh children, near Dolgellau, 1860

Outside our own door we had an amusing encounter with a troop of small boys, in all varieties of costume and patches. They were all more or less ragged, but with such happy mischievous faces, and looking so roguish as they all pressed round us, teazing & bothering for halfpennies, that they were quite irresistible, & we held up a penny before them all (much as one would a bit of meat to a dog when one wants to make it beg) & after keeping them some time in suspense, tossed it in amongst the group, & let them scramble for it. It was such an amusing sight, that we went on throwing pennies until all our store was exhausted, & throwing silver being too expensive a form of amusement, we left the children to fight out the possession of the last penny, & went on into the house. Nothing more

happened that night, and Gertrude and I spent the evening sketching the group of children, both which sketches I enter here, as they are quite different views of the same subject.

*115* Diary of Frederica St John Rouse-Boughton, 1860.   Bedfordshire Record Office,   OR 2244/5   (**25**)

# Antique Ruins

*Although many diarists were widely read and evidently scholars, few seem to have been knowledgeable antiquarians. Thus, visits to the remains of ancient castles, abbeys and other ruins were as likely to prompt philosophical reflections and flights of romantic fancy as much as genuine historical enquiry. Cathedrals were objects of much interest but parish churches seem scarcely to be noticed.*

## Stonehenge in 1747

We dined in the Town of Amesbury and went on to Stonehenge which lies near it. By whom and for what use this was built or what machines could even move such immense stones has puzzled, and still puzzles all that see it. The stones stand in a Circular form, there are between 60 and 70 of them. There is the remains of a ditch round them with four entrances, some of the stones are 22 ft. high and seven wide.

*116*   Diary of Sophia, Lady Newdigate, 1747.   Warwickshire Record Office,   CR.1841/7   **(566)**

*117*   A View of Part of Stonehenge, by Sophia, Lady Newdigate, 1747. Warwickshire Record Office,   CR.1841/7   **(566)**

## Stonehenge in 1779

About 1 m. from the western Boundary of the Park stands Stonehenge, that Wonderful and inexplicable object of Curiosity. it is seated on a natural Eminence nor higher than some others. it is difficult to count the Pieces, nor is it of much consequence. they are of very different sizes, The largest I guess, 30 F. high, 7 or 8 broad, and 5 or 6 thick, some of them have perhaps been broken by their Fall. Time has operated variously upon them; some being split, some farrowed, others worn into several irregular Cavities, they all appear of very great Antiquity, their Angles being every where worn quite obtuse. though in general they appear not to have been subjected to Tools; yet the round Prominences which are visible upon the Tops of some of the Jambs, which were to receive the Imposts with their corresponding cavities, must have been the work of Art. though it is impossible to say, how these vast Masses were brought hither and set up, and whence they were taken, yet I am inclined to think they are not the work of Art, as has been imagined.

*118* Diary of Sir John Cullum, 1779. Suffolk Record Office, Bury St Edmunds, E2/33/2 **(539)**

## Ludlow Castle, 1755

Ludlow is an handsome town and has an old Castle now in a neglected and ruinous state, but which by its remains appears to have been once a very strong fortress and an habitation very equal to the power and dignity of the Lord President of Wales, who resided there. Not far from this town is Okeley Park belonging to my Lord Powis, and part of that forest which Milton in his Masque supposes to have been inhabited by Comus and his rout. The God is now vanished, but at the revolution of every 7 years his rout do not fail to keep orgies there and in the neighbouring city; as Lord Powis knows to his cost, for he has spent £20,000 or £30,000 in entertaining them at those seasons which is the reason that he has no house at this place fit for him to live in. He talks of building one in the park and the situation deserves it . . .

*119* Diary of Sir George Lyttelton, 5th Bt, 1755. Clwyd Record Office, D/E/1209 **(52)**

*120* Ludlow Castle, 1774

## Kirkstall Abbey, Leeds, 1796

While at Leeds I made frequent Visits to Kirkstall Abbey, that noble Pile of Monastic Remains, which is exceeded by few perhaps in the Kingdom. In my former Tour I gave a sketch or two of the magnificent Ruins, but being more at leisure I accumulated my stock. . . . The opposite view is the aspect which it presents towards Leeds.

*121* Diary of Rev John Swete, 1796. Devon Record Office, MS 2 **(112)**

*122* Eastern View of Kirkstall Abbey, watercolour by Rev John Swete, 1796. Devon Record Office, MS2 **(112)**

## Llanthony Abbey, near Abergavenny, 1804

August 7th, Tuesday. Hired a horse and set out at six this Morning for Lantony Abbey; it is distant about twelve miles from Abergavenny; after riding near four miles on the Road to Hereford, you turn off to the left into a Lane, and in a short time you come near the Munnow a small Stream here, and keeping it on your right hand, the Road follows its winding course thro' a most romantic Country, sometimes on the side of the Mountains and at others in the valley beside it – the valley thro' which it runs is narrow and inclosed on both sides with a Chain of Mountains which vary their form at almost every step – the rattling of this Stream sometimes near you and sometimes at a distance over its little Falls and Banks of Stone and Pebbles, adds very much to the effect of the Scenery – after a winding road of about seven Miles you cross the Stream by a Bridge of one small Arch and soon come in sight of the Abbey – it is a beautiful Ruin, originally in the form of a Cross – its form, and situation at the side of the valley, the Stream running in the bottom, the bold mountains on each side, and others in the background partly lost in the hazy distance was a sight which amply compensated for travelling on a very bad road to it – the Abbey now belongs to Col. Wood, who is fitting up a part of it to render it habitable – N.B. The Angel at Abergavenny a very bad Inn, every thing dirty and disgusting and the Landlady very imposing.

*123* Diary of Robert Parker FSA, 1804. Hampshire Record Office, 18M51/557 (**263**)

*124* Llanthony Abbey, drawn by Robert Parker FSA, 1804. Hampshire Record Office, 18M51/557 (**263**)

## Carreg Cennen Castle, 1804

August 9th, Thursday, Llandilo Vawr. Hired a horse and set out at seven in the Morning for Carrick Kennin Castle, about four miles from Llandilo Vawr; the road is over the Bridge to the Turnpike and then immediately to the left up the side of a steep Hill, over Rocks and rolling Stones, to a lofty Tree which is the halfway and visible as well from Llandilo as from the Castle; it forms a complete Landmark so that tho' you may wander you cannot be lost, from this Tree the Castle is in sight, and as you approach it, it has the gloomy stateliness of the old Barons times – it is situate upon an insulated Rock, having a sloping acclivity to the West, and a Precipice to the East and South, the Approach to the Entrance seems to have been on the North Side; the views from hence are fine, for it is surrounded with the Welch mountains. To the East you look over the Black mountn. into Glamorganshire – (the Black Mountain runs from Abergavenny north to near Llandavan Forge late Mr. Vaughans of Golden Grove), whose Park you see on the South and Cardiganshire on the West – Under this Castle is a Gallery of considerable extent hewn out of the Rock into which you are conducted by an Old Welch Woman with a Rush-light – the water which filters thro' the Rock, is caught in a little hollow in this Gallery, and is considered as a Specifick for weak Eyes – a little Welch boy without shoes or Stockings and without a syllable of English, conducted me along a winding Path to the bottom of this Eminence, from whence I had a view of this Castle in all its Grandeur, looking up to it from the valley over which it hangs from the Edge of the Precipice. Whilst I admired the Scene, my little Guide amused himself with gathering and eating green Nuts and green

*126*   Carreg Cennen Castle, drawn by Robert Parker FSA,
1804.   Hampshire Record Office,   18M51/557   (**263**)

Sloes – the Path winds round the Castle and brings you to the Cottage of the old woman. I was invited and went in; the best room is about six feet long and four wide the floor is of Earth, except the hearth which is of stone – she offered me Oaten Cake with Butter and Milk, the latter I took and it was extremely rich and served with much neatness.

*125* Diary of Robert Parker, FSA, 1804. Hampshire Record Office, 18M51/557 (**263**)

## Greenstead Church, Essex, 1809

April 20th. Breakfasted at Ongar. Drove to Grinstead Church built intirely of Logs of Wood, a very great piece of antiquity. Could not see inside as the clerk lived a mile and a half from the Church.

*127* Diary of Millicent Bant, 1809. Essex Record Office, D/DFr F4 (**184**)

*128* Greenstead Church, early 19th century. Essex Record Office

# London

*Visits to the capital are recorded in some ninety diaries. For the well-to-do, the gentry and the sophisticated visitor, these provided opportunities for renewing old acquaintances, for social engagements, for theatregoing and the like, and it was left to the country cousins to record visits to historical sights and tourist attractions. These diaries offer yet another perspective of London life from the eighteenth century.*

## The opening night of Ireland's 'Vortigern' at Drury Lane Theatre, 3 April 1796

The scene at Drury Lane last night was in all respects novel to me; the house itself was an agreeable surprize for tho' very large it was not so large as I had painted it to myself, but it is admirably contrived and I am told holds 3,000 persons, it was quite full even to crowd, yet we should have heard well, on a common occasion, as we were situated in one of the centre boxes of the first row . . . but this was not a common occasion; the house however were very well disposed to give it a fair hearing, and tho' the person who was to speak the Prologue was so flatter'd that he cou'd not proceed after some contest he was suffer'd to read it. It modestly begg'd the attention of the audience to the Play and expressed acquiescence in their judgement whatever it may be. The three first acts were tolerably quiet, tho' at times there were efforts made by the adverse party to stop its proceeding, yet there was a most decisive majority in favour of its being heard. In the beginning of the fourth act the disapprobation became more general, but the bursts of laughter that some passages produced (for what shou'd be great was farce) made it a good humour'd disapprobation. However the symptoms were such that Mr. Ireland, who sat within one box of us, made off.

. . . After much difficulty silence was procured and the play went on, not, however without great interruption in almost every speech; but when Mr. Kemble who acted Vortigern (and seem'd to do his best, tho' I am told against his own feelings) said "It's time this solemn mockery were ended" the uproar exceeded everything I cou'd have imagin'd, after numberless vain attempts he went on, but for one line only before the bursts of laughter, clapping, hissing etc. were renewed, and in this manner a speech of a few lines was, at least, a quarter of an hour in speaking . . . when it was attempted to be given out for another representation, the disapprobation was so decided that it was given up, not however without a violent struggle from the party in its favour particularly one gentleman in stage box (Mr. Sturt, I am told, a member of Parliament) who throughout the representation made himself very conspicuous, making many efforts to jump upon the stage from which he was withheld by his friends; . . .

From what I heard of this Play and I heard the first part very well, I find no trait of Shakspear throughout; Mr. Telford, who call'd just now, said with true zeal for Shakspear "Had I found a play that I knew to be his, if it wou'd not have added to his reputation, I wou'd not have produc'd it."

*129* Diary of Katherine Plymley, 1796. Shropshire Record Office, 567/5/5/1/10 **(485)**

## High society in London, 1802

April 29. We went with the Wyldes to the Smyrna Coffee House to see peace proclaimed at St James's; the Queen, Princesses, and Princess Charlotte at Lady C. Finche's windows; the heralds in their dress on horseback with numbers of noblemen proceeded down Pall Mall, the Strand, and Temple Bar, where they were met by the Lord Mayor (Mr Eamer) (who was an apprentice in Nottingham to Mr Alderman Butler, a grocer in the Market Place).

June 3. We were at Madam Mara's concert at the opera house with C.R. and Mr Thomas Smith; most highly delighted, the first performers in the kingdom, a duet between Madam Mara and Mrs Billington; the last time of Mara's performance as she is going abroad.

4. The dear king's birthday; we in the park at the time the guns were firing, a most lovely day; went to Mrs Story's in St James' Street to see the nobility go to court, spent the day with her as did C.R; we all walked to see the illuminations at night.

17. Mr Wylde took us to a room in St James's Palace where we saw the queen, five princesses pass through with the lords-in-waiting to the drawing room; they all had the same dress as at the king's birthday; most superbly dressed and all looking remarkably well, Princess Elizabeth most pleasing, good natured countenance; saw his Majesty pass through another room, he looked in good health and spirits.

18, Mrs S. Smith and Miss Turner called to take leave; they are going to Woodhall for the summer; Captain R. went with us and Mr Davy to Vauxhall; Lord and Lady Castlereagh and a prodigious number of nobility there; the fireworks beautiful, Mrs Bland and the music enchanting and the tout ensemble the most delightful; we stayed till near 3 o'c(lock).

Jul 20. We at a review and sham fight on Wimbledon Common, the Prince and Duke of York; had a full view of their highnesses, much delighted; in the evening at half past 9 o'c(lock) we went to Vauxhall; extremely full, three thousand people; a fire balloon conducted by Garnerin and fireworks by Signor Ruggieri; we supped there and returned at 3 o'c(lock), C.R. and Davy with us; highly amused.

21 At the British Museum; Dr Gray attended us, a cross, disagreeable looking man; saw immense curiosities; in the evening at the little theatre 'The Heiress' and 'The Review'; much entertained with the play.

*130*   Diary of Abigail Gawthern, 1802.   Nottinghamshire Record Office,   M23,904   **(464)**

## The Emperor of Prussia at St Paul's, 1814

16 June. Went into Town in the Stage to be present at the Anniversary meeting of the Charity Children at St Paul's. Stood at the Gate about ¾ of an hour and then rushed into the Church. Our Party were the first in. At ½ past eleven the Emperor, attended by Ld Yarmouth, entered the Cathedral. Here his Majesty witnessed the annual assemblage of from eight to ten thousand Children belonging to the different Parishes of the Metropolis, an interesting sight which does so much honour to British benevolence & which cannot fail to make the most affecting impression on every beholder. His Prussian Majesty & the Princes his Sons were of the Party after the Service was ended. The Church resounded with the acclamations & cheers of the People which were in the whole, it is supposed, near 30,000. On some person exclaiming long live the Emperor, he went immediately from his seat to the gallery under the Organ, where the whole assemblage had a full view of him. We then dined at our favorite shrimp shop and walked home.

*131*   Diary of Hannah Abbott, 1814. Dorset Record Office, D.43/F15 **(129)**

# Visit to the Great Exhibition, 1851

London, October 1851. In once more passing through the avenues and galleries, I discovered an infinite number of things worthy of study that I had before overlooked, and if I were to go a dozen times more, I should doubtless continue to discover many more that have, even now, escaped my notice. This is not strange in a place so large, and filled with such a vast and such a varied collection. Before I came out I took another look at the Koh-i-Noor Diamond, worth between two and three millions of money: and I tried the gravity of the policeman on duty, by the side of the Cage in which it is kept, and with all the simplicity I could assume, by asking – Whether the public were allowed to handle that article? Also took another glance at the Queen of Spain's jewels, the spirited group of sculpture "The Amazon" by Kiss (the German with the ridiculous name); at most of the other objects of sculpture; at the machinery; the wood carving; the furniture; the carpets; the tapestry; the glass; the silver and gold plate; the naval models; the piano-fortes, and other musical instruments; the cutlery; the china; the watch and clock work – in short, I looked all round and admired everywhere, for everything is good in its way.

*132*  Diary of Peter Orlando Hutchinson, 1851.   Devon Record
Office,   MS 36   (**119**)

*133*   Sketch of the Crystal Palace, 14 October 1851.   Devon Record
Office,   MS 36   (**119**)

'A "Bloomer" as she appeared in Kensington Garden on Sunday afternoon the 28th of September, 1851. A brazen face creature!'

134   Diary of Peter Orlando Hutchinson, 1851.   Devon Record Office,   MS 36   (**119**)

# Visit to the Festival Gardens, Battersea, 6 June 1951

The weather has turned into glorious summer with midday temperatures in the 70's. London looks gay in this festival year with the sun beaming on the beflowered gardens and the flags which flutter from every public and office building.

We went to the Festival Gardens at Battersea the other evening. Unexpectedly they were not too crowded – it was a fine evening – and we were able to walk around comfortably. First through the Fun Fair which was noisy and full of activity with the great dipper, wall of death, the Rotor, an affair which with a rapidly whirling floor dropping away from the victims leaves them suspended against the circular walls – ship, roundabouts, rifle ranges, fortune tellers and the rest. Next to the lake and fountains with their myriad lights and on to the Riverside walk with gay shops of varying styles of architecture but all light and fairy. Overall are flood lights making pageant of the London plane trees. At 11pm the fireworks blaze away and the rockets burst high up in the night sky to fall in coloured rain on the gardens below. A very enjoyable experience. One discordant note was the large amount of litter under the tables in the restaurants and floating on the lake.

*135*　Diary of Leslie Todd, 1951.　Surrey Record Office,　2830/1/25　(**563**)

*136*　'Nellie' the Engine, the Far Tottering and Oystercreek Railway, Festival Gardens, Festival of Britain 1951

# The End

I have told my story of these travels and junketings, and therefore, having in this respect fulfilled my duty, I, the Editor, properly tired with so many days of roaming and rambling, retire to bed, and wish you GOOD NIGHT.

137   Diary of Elizabeth Palmer, 1871.   Hampshire Record Office, 9M68/63   (**271**)

# Catalogue of Diaries

*Catalogue of Diaries of Travel in England, Wales and Scotland deposited in the County Record Offices of England and Wales, with Indexes of Diarists and Places*

The catalogue identifies each separate original home travel diary in the fifty County Record Offices of England and Wales. The diaries are listed by county of deposit in alphabetical order and are numbered in one sequence. Within each county the diaries are listed in chronological order, except that those of a single person or family are kept together.

The range of detail in each diary precludes any indication of subject content, while the territorial coverage is restricted mainly to the counties and to principal towns when these were the main object of the journeys. In some cases, too, only the country or general area is given, and in others merely the terminal points of the journey. The present administrative counties are used for both England and Wales, except that the former counties of Hereford, Worcester and Huntingdon are retained. The identification of places in Scotland is mostly generalised.

The sequence of each entry is as follows: catalogue number; name and any details of diarist; counties, places or areas visited; year of journey; the number of volumes if more than one; the approximate size of volumes; number of pages; if illustrated; and, finally, the document reference number. The index is confined to names of diarists and to place names in the catalogue only.

The catalogue is intended principally as a checklist and guide, and intending researchers are advised to write to the County Archivist of the county in question for further details of and access to any diary included.

# Bedfordshire

Bedfordshire Record Office, County Hall
Bedford, MK42 9AP

**1** *Jemima, Marchioness Grey* of Wrest Park
(1722–1797): Northants 1743; Bucks, Northants
1748, crown 4to, 27pp. (L 30/9a/1)

**2** *do.* Warws, Staffs, Oxon, Bucks, Cambs
1748; Cambs, Suff, Norf 1750; N Yorks 1752;
Edinburgh, Dunkeld, Berwick 1755, crown 4to,
42pp. (L 30/9a/2)

**3** *do.* Surr, Berks 1760, crown 4to, 7pp.
(L 30/9a/3)

**4** *do.* Kent 1746, crown 4to, 8pp. (L 30/9a/4)

**5** *do.* Bucks, Northants, Staffs, Warws, Oxon,
Cambs 1748; Wilts, Som 1749, crown 4to, 55pp.
(L 30/9a/5)

**6** *do.* Cambs, Suff, Norf 1750; Surr 1751; N
Yorks 1752; Surr, Berks 1754, crown 4to, 32pp.
(L 30/9a/6)

**7** *do.* Cambs, Suff, Norf (cf 6) 1750, 4to, 12pp.
(L 30/21/3/9)

**8** *do.* Surr, Notts, Yorks, Durham, Northumb,
Edinburgh, Lothian, Tayside 1755; Berks 1760,
crown 4to, 88pp. (L 30/9a/7)

**9** *do.* Northern tour (cf 8) 1755, 4to, 28pp.
(L 30/21/3/10)

**10** *do.* Norf, Cambs 1762; Som, Worcs, Staffs,
Derbys 1763; London, Surr, E Suss 1764, 4to,
81pp. (L 30/9a/8)

**11** *do.* S Yorks, Hunts 1767; Bucks 1769; crown
4to, 25pp. (L 30/9a/9)

**12** *Christian Russell* of Westminster (1714–
1803): Wilts, Devon, Corn 1760–1761; Som
1761–1762; Hants 1762; Derbys 1763; 4to, 55pp.
(M 10/2/131–144, 165, 246, pp.155–6)

**13** *Alexander Hume-Campbell, Lord Polworth* of
Mertoun (1750–1781): London to and from
Scotland (journey times, distances, accounts),
1772–1774, 8vo, 18pp. (L 31/110)

**14** *Constantia Orlebar* of Hinwick (1739–1808):
Northants, Leics, Derbys 1776, 4to, 24pp.
(OR 2194)

**15** *John Higgins* of Turvey (1768–1846): Beds,
Northants, Warws, Worcs, Glos, Gwent 1796,
crown 4to, 3pp. (HG 12/3/7)

**16** *Thomas Philip, 3rd Lord Grantham* of Newby
& Wrest, Earl de Grey (from 1833) (1781–1859):
W Yorks, S Yorks 1797, crown 4to, 14pp.
(L 31/114/1)

**17** *do.* Oxford, Oxon, Warws, Worcs, Salop,
Staffs, Ches, Lancs, Derbys, Yorks 1799, 2vols,
8vo, 96pp, 88pp, illus. with sketches of
machinery). (L 31/114/2,3)

**18** *do.* yachting trip from Cowes to Plymouth,
incl visits ashore Devon, Corn 1813, 12mo,
64pp. (L 31/114/6)

**19** *do.* Edinburgh to Inverness, then by yacht
Caledonian Canal, Inner Hebrides, N Scotland
1829, 4to, 112 pp, with map of route. (L 31/114/
10)

**20** *Lady Henrietta Cole* (*Lady Grantham* 1805,
Lady de Grey 1833) (1784–1848): Holyhead to
Yorks 1803, 8vo, 12pp. (L 31/111)

**21** *Lady Emma Maria Elizabeth St John* of
Melchbourne (1762–1825): Mid Wales 1811, 8vo,
3pp. (W 1/3090)

**22** *Ann Bletchley* of Newington Green (1790–
1856): Wye Valley, S Wales 1812, 4to, 51pp.
(SY 46)

**23** *George Duncombe* of London (1783–?1865):
Suss, Dorset, Devon 1821, crown 4to, 2pp.
(Z 462/3)

**24** *Mary Ann Brooks* of Flitwick (1822–1848):
Kent, Surr, Berks 1843; Cambridge 1844;
Chester, Liverpool, Ches 1845; N Wales,
Chester, Liverpool 1847, crown 4to, 28pp.
(LL 19/2)

**25** *Frederica St John Rouse-Boughton* of Larden
Hall (Salop) (1838–1928): N Wales, Herefs,
Salop 1860; Beds, Northants, Berks 1861, crown
4to, 168pp, illus. (OR 2244/5)

**26** *do.* Lake District, Scotland, Salop 1861;
Salop 1862; crown 4to, 130pp, illus. (OR 2244/6)

**27** *do.* Salop, Mid Wales, Aberystwyth 1863;
Worcs, Warws 1864; crown 4to, 60pp, illus.
(OR 2244/7)

**28** *Emily Starey* of Highgate (1851–1924):
Folkestone, Canterbury 1871; Folkestone 1872;
N Wales 1874; I of W 1875; Streatham 1875,
1878, 4to, 348pp. (SY 235)

**29** *Mary Louisa Smyth* of Edworth (1868–1954):
Salisbury 1905; Cliftonville 1906; Folkestone
1907; Felixstowe, London 1908; Scotland 1909;
Lyme Regis 1910; Lake District 1911; N Wales
1912; Scotland 1913; Cromer, St Leonards on
Sea, Herefs 1914; Torquay 1915; Bude 1916; 8vo,
70pp. (SM/E 54)

**30** *Gregory J M Whyley* of Bedford (b. 1881): on
yacht *Naucrates* on R. Ouse from Bedford to
Huntingdon, with excursions 1897, 8vo, 47pp.
(Z 589/4)

## Berkshire
Berkshire Record Office, Shire Hall, Shinfield Park, Reading, RG2 9XD

**31** *Edward Belson* of Reading: London, Berks 1707–09, 21mo, 35pp. (D/EX12/1)

**32** *(John?) Mount* of London and Wasing: Kent 1759, fo, 3pp. (D/EMt/F5)

**33** *John Mount* jnr, of Wasing: Devon, Hants 1782; Birmingham, Glos, Worcs, Warws 1799, 6to, 17pp. (D/EMt/F6)

**34** *Anon* (Mount family of Wasing): Kent 1808, 8vo, 32pp. (D/EMt/F7)

**35** T E Mount (schoolboy) of Basingstoke: Dorset, Southampton 1840, 2vols, 8vo, 15pp. (D/EMt/F18/2,3)

**36** *Anon* (Wilder family of Sulham and Purley): voyage S Coast, Channel Islands, coach from Polperro to Southampton 1793, 8vo, 59pp. (D/EWi/F2)

**37** *Anon* (Pleydell-Bouverie family of Coleshill): London to Edinburgh and return to Wilts 1794, 4to, 16pp. (D/EPb/F27)

**38** *Mrs Price*: Devon, Som 1805, 4to, 40pp. (D/EEg/Z1)

**39** *Anon* (Palmer or Ewen family of Sonning): Cambs, Notts, Yorks, Lake District, Lancs, Liverpool, Ches, Derbys, Staffs, Warws, Northants 1835, 4to, 15pp. (D/EE/Z26)

## Buckinghamshire
Buckinghamshire Record Office, County Hall, Aylesbury, HP20 1UA

No relevant diaries

## Cambridgeshire
Cambridgeshire Record Office, Shire Hall, Cambridge, CB3 0AP

**40** *Rev Townley Clarkson*: Norf, Suff, Essex, Kent, Surr, Berks, Oxon, Warws, Staffs, Ches, Lancs, Cumb, Scotland, Northumb, Yorks, Derbys, Leics, Northants, Hunts 1804, 8vo, 85pp. (R57/11/1)

**41** *do*. Hunts, Leics, Salop, Wales, Ches, Lancs, Yorks, Derbys, Northants 1808, 8vo, 50pp. (R57/11/1)

**42** *do*. Herts, Essex, Kent, Surr 1810, 8vo, 16pp. (R57/11/1)

**43** *do*. Suff 1811, 8vo, 4pp. (R57/11/1)

**44** *do*. Essex, Hunts, Beds, Bucks, Herts 1811, 8vo, 2pp. (R57/11/1)

**45** *do*. Herts, London 1811, 8vo, 2pp. (R57/11/1)

**46** *Lady Philadelphia Cotton* of Madingley: Hunts, Northants, Warws, Worcs 1818, 8vo, 23pp. (588/F48)

**47** *do*. Warws, Salop, Wales 1819, 8vo, 12pp. (588/F48)

Huntingdonshire Record Office, Grammar School Walk, Huntingdon, PE18 6LF

**48** *George Thornhill* of Diddington: Northants, Lincs, Notts, Yorks, Durham, Northumb, Scotland, Cumb, Lancs 1760, 12mo, 31pp. (148/5/274)

## Cheshire
Cheshire Record Office, Duke Street, Chester, CH1 1RL

**49** *Sir John Thomas Stanley, 1st Baron Stanley* (1766–1850): Som 1804, 8vo, 81pp, illus. (DSA 5/7). Part published in Jane H Adeane, *The Early Married Life of Maria Josepha, Lady Stanley*, 2nd edn, 1900, pp.173–274.

**50** *Anon* ('W M'): Ches 1813; Lake District 1817; Wye Valley 1833, 8vo, 68pp. (DDX 224)

**51** *Elizabeth Mary Barnard*: London, Ches, Staffs, Warws 1858, 8vo, 24pp. (DDX 459)

## Cleveland
Cleveland Archives Department, Exchange Buildings, 6 Marton Road, Middlesborough, TS1 1DB

No relevant diaries.

## Clwyd
Clwyd Record Office, The Old Rectory, Hawarden, Deeside, CH5 3NR

**52** *Sir George Lyttelton, 5th Bt, 1st Lord Lyttelton*: Salop, N Wales 1755, 4to, 16pp. (D/E/1209)

**53** *Philp Yorke* of Erddig (d.1803): N Wales 1766, 4to, 30pp. (D/E/1209)

**54** *Elizabeth Giffard* of Nerquis Hall: Nerquis to Bath, Bristol 1766–1767, 8vo, 62pp. (D/NH/1074)

**55**   *do.* Ches, Salop, Staffs 1767, 8vo, 2pp. (D/NH/1075)

**56**   *do.* Ches, Clwyd, Salop, Staffs, Warws, Oxon, Berks, London 1773, 8vo, 20pp. (D/NH/1076)

**57**   *do.* rough draft of 56, 8vo, 6pp. (D/NH/1077)

**58**   *Thomas Pennant* (1726–1798): Derbys, Yorks, Notts, Lincs, Herts 1786; Berks, Wilts, Devon, Dorset, Hants 1787; Berks, Wilts, Glos, Worcs 1788, 8vo, 6pp. (D/NA/850)

**59**   *Richard G Francis* of Norfolk (c.1830–1912): Chester, N Wales 1851, 8vo, 87pp. (D/DM/538/1)

Ruthin Branch Office

**60**   *Anon:* Ches, Salop, N Wales 1808, 4to, 69pp, illus. (DD/DM/228/78)

**61**   *Sarah Brinkley:* N Wales, Salop, Staffs, Warws, Oxon, Berks, London 1822, 8vo, 26pp. (DD/PR/133)

**62**   *do.* Scotland 1823, 8vo, 43pp. (DD/PR/134)

**64**   *Mrs Brinkley?:* Scotland 1823, 8vo, 25pp. (DD/PR/135)

**64**   *William Graeme Tomkins* of London: Warws, Staffs, Salop, Derbys, Manchester, Liverpool, N Wales 1834, 8vo, 60pp. (DD/DM/365/1)

# Cornwall
Cornwall Record Office, County Hall, Truro, TR1 3AY

**65**   *Rev Joshua Howell* (1698–1785): Visit to London 1732, 8vo, 54pp. (HL (2) 193)

**66**   *William Wynne* (1692–1765): London to Cornwall and back 1755, 4vo, 30pp. (PD 220). Cornish section published in *Journal of the Royal Institution of Cornwall*, New Series, Vol VIII, Pt 4, 1981.

**67**   *Anon:* Norf, Suff 1757, 8vo, 20pp. (HL (2) 593)

**68**   *Luttrell Wynne* (1738–1814): Oxon, Birmingham, Warws, Staffs, Derbys 1771, 8vo, 46pp, illus. (PD 464)

**69**   *do.* Derbys, Ches, Clwyd 1771, 8vo, 68pp, illus. (PD 465)

**70**   *do.* Sketchbook: Corn, Devon, Oxon, Derbys, Warws 1771 (PD 439)

**71**   *do.* N Wales 1771, 8vo, 76pp. (PD 466)

**72**   *do.* N Wales 1771, 8vo, 70pp. (PD 467)

**73**   *do.* Sketchbook: N Wales 1771 (PD 434)

**74**   *do.* S Wales 1773, 8vo, 76pp, illus. (PD 469)

**75**   *do.* Oxford, Shrewsbury, N Wales, Chester, Warws 1774, 8vo, 63pp, illus. (PD 470)

**76**   *do.* S Wales 1793, 8vo, 70pp, illus. (PD 468)

**77**   *John Enys* (1757–1818): Lake District, Scotland 1783, 8vo, 265pp. (EN 1800)

**78**   *do.* Yorks, Lake District 1783, 4to, 18pp. (EN 1802)

**79**   *do.* Lake District, Scotland 1783, 4to, 19pp. (EN 1803)

**80**   *do.* Scotland 1783, 4to, 33pp. (EN 1804)

**81**   *do.* Scotland, Yorks 1783, 4to, 36pp. (EN 1805)

**82**   *do.* Yorks to London, Wilts, Som to Corn 1783, 4to, 26pp. (EN 1806)

**83**   *Anon:* Corn to Birmingham via Som, Oxford, Warwick, and back via Monmouth, Gloucester, Som, Devon 1785, 8vo, 73pp. (T 1341/1,2)

**84**   *Mr Guillebard* (?): London to Corn and back 1795, 8vo, 150pp (AD 43). Cornish section published by Kingston Publications, Mevagissey, 1971.

**85**   *Rachel Stackhouse* (1777–1813): Bath, Salisbury 1800, 8vo, 32pp. (R (S) 1/174)

**86**   *Mary Boger:* Plymouth to Corn 1814, 4to, 14pp. (BG 104)

**87**   *Fanny Russell* (1799–1847): London 1814, 8vo, 35pp. (HL (2) 379)

**88**   *Charles Valentine le Grice* (1773–1858): England, Wales, Scotland 1826, 8vo, 75pp. (X 20/40)

**89**   *do.* London, Liverpool, Oxford, Exeter 1829, 8vo, 94pp. (X 30/41)

**90**   *Anon:* Corn 1885, 8vo, 66pp, illus. (AD 72/9). Published by Kingston Publications, Mevagissey, 1971.

# Cumbria
Cumbria Record Office, The Castle, Carlisle, CA3 8UR

**91**   *Christopher Lowther:* Scotland 1629, 8vo, 64pp. (D/Lons/L2/4). Published by David Douglas, Edinburgh, 1894.

**92**   *Henry Curwen:* Ride from Workington to Barnet 1726, 8vo, 5pp. (D/Cu.1/7)

**93** *Anon* (Quaker missionary): Scotland 1787, 4to, 75pp. (DX/38/69)

**94** *Anon*: Scotland 1800, 3 vols, 4to, 62pp, 63pp, 62pp. (D/RW2–4)

**95** *Mary Ferguson*: Allonby 1820, 12mo, 31pp. (DX/249/17)

**96** *Henry Howard*: London to Greystoke and Carlisle, Lake District 1821, 8vo, 47pp. (D/HW8/5)

Cumbria Record Office, County Offices, Kendal, LA9 4RQ

**97** *Anon*: London to Newcastle upon Tyne by sea, Northumb, Cumb 1801, 8vo, 27pp. (WD/MG)

**98** *Anon*: Lake District 1871, 4to, 22pp. (WD/K)

**99** *Henry Walker* of Windermere: Walking and cycling tours, England, Scotland 1899–1915, 4to, 150pp. (WDX/141)

Cumbria Record Office, 140 Duke Street, Barrow-in-Furness, LA14 1XW

**100** *Sir William Gell* (1777–1836): Lake District 1797, 4to, 105pp, illus. (Z 293). Published by F Graham, Newcastle upon Tyne, 1968.

**101** *Rev W Shepherd*: Lake District 1804, crown 4to, 42pp, illus. (Z 198)

**102** *Anon* (Gurney or Cockfield families): Lake District c.1805, crown 4to, 20pp. (BDX/59/2)

## Derbyshire
Derbyshire Record Office, Education Department, County Offices, Matlock, DE4 3AG

**103** *Anon* (Strutt family?): Staffs, Warws, Glos, Som, Devon, Dorset, Berks, London, Cambs, Lincs, Derbys 1814–15, 2 vols, 8vo, 68pp, 18pp. (D2943M/F1/1–2)

**104** *do.* London, Herts, Derbys 1831, 8vo, 18pp. (D2943M/F2/1)

**105** *do.* Lake District 1849, 8vo, 74pp. (D2943M/F6/1)

**106** *George Crewe*: I of Wight (extracts) 1817–18, 12mo, 37pp, illus. (D2375M/180/23)

**107** *Isabel Adderley*: Wales 1868, 12mo, 37pp, illus. (D2375M/180/20)

## Devon
Devon Record Office, Castle Street, Exeter, EX4 3PU

**108** *Anon* (Hoblyn family): Cornwall to Som 1741, 12mo, 5pp. (64/12/29/13)

**109** *Sarah England*: Buxton, Derbys 1793, 8vo, 40pp. (337B/14/1(4/3a))

**110** *William George Maton*: Dorset, Devon, Corn 1794, 4to, 2 vols, 113pp, 94pp, illus. (MS1). Printed in *Tour of Western Counties*, 1797.

**111** *Rev John Swete* (1752–1821): S Devon 1788, 4to, 88pp, illus. (MS2)

**112** *do.* N Devon 1789, 4to, 121pp, illus. (MS2)

**113** *do.* Corn, Notts, Derbys c.1790, 4to, 192pp, illus. (MS2). Cornish section published in *Journal of Royal Institution of Cornwall*, ed. Rosemary Leach, New Series, Vol VI, Pt 3, 1971, pp.185–219.

**114** *do.* Notts, W Yorks c.1796, 4to, 59pp, illus. (MS2)

**115** *do.* Devon, Corn, 1789–1801, 17 vols, 4to, resp. 230, 217, 192, 195, 193, 187, 190, 195, 193, 201, 212, 187, 189, 191, 189, 193pp. (564M/F1–17). Extracts and some illus in *Devons Age of Elegance*, ed. Peter Hunt, Devon Books, 1987.

**116** *do.* S Wales 1791, N Devon 1794, 8vo, 139pp. illus. (2693M/F1)

**117** *Hugh Fortescue* (later 2nd Earl Fortescue) (1783–1859): Wales 1808, 4to, 23pp. (1262M/FD5)

**118** *John Farrant* (?): Scotland (Highlands), Lake District 1831, 8vo, 41pp. (2933M/26)

**119** *Peter Orlando Hutchinson* (1810–1897): London, incl. Great Exhibition 1851, 8vo, 32pp (part), illus (separate vol). (MS36)

**120** *James Wentworth Buller* (1798–1865): London, Yorks 1853, 8vo, 5pp. (2065M/F9/41)

**121** *do.* Lake District 1861, 8vo, 5pp. (2065M/F9/42)

**122** *do.* Anon (Torr family): Corn, Lake District 1853, 12mo, 21pp, 14pp. (M36)

**123** *do.* (Torr family): Suss 1862, 8vo, 60pp. (MS36)

**124** *do.* Devon 1856, 8vo, 80pp. (MS36)

**125** *do.* (Proby family): Lake District 1859, 16mo, 11pp. (337addB/MF83/2)

**126** *do.* (Proby family): Great Exhibition, Kent 1862, 16mo, 9pp. (337addB/MF83/3)

## Dorset

Dorset Record Office, County Hall, Dorchester, DT1 1XJ

**127** *Andrew Abbott*: Som, Dorset, Wilts 1798, 4to, 4pp. (D.43/F30)

**128** *Mrs T Rackett*: Devon, Corn 1802, fo, 4pp. (D.1/NU 140)

**129** *Hannah Abbott* (1788–1873): London 1814, 4to, 12pp. (D.43/F15)

**130** *Harriet Colfox* (1783–1851): London 1818–1819, 4to, 8pp. (D.43/F11)

**131** *Charles Weld* (1812–1885): Scottish Highlands 1832, 4to, 12pp. (D.16/F19)

**132** *Elizabeth Syndercombe Bower*: W Country, Midlands, N England, Lake District, Wales 1837, 8vo, 141pp. (D.1/KW 209)

**133** *Jane Mary Elizabeth Deane* (1834–1843): Oxford 1840, 8vo, 24pp. (D.359/F 20 A)

**134** *Charles Edward Oakley* (d.1865): Scottish Highlands 1851, 4to, 28pp. (D.320/F62)

**135** *Nigel Bond*: Suff 1920, fo, 8pp. (D.413/Box 23)

## Durham

Durham Record Office, County Hall, Durham, DH1 5UL

**136** *W Stobart* of Pelaw: Leeds 1799, 8vo, 39pp. (D/X 495/3)

**137** *William Bernard Ogden* (d.1870): Durham, London 1814–1822, 4 vols, crown 4to, 95pp, 129pp, 139pp, 109pp. (D/X 782/1–4)

**138** *John Buddle* (1773–1843): London 1833, 8vo, 33pp. (D/X 563/1)

**139** *Francis P Cockshutt* of Shildon: Teesdale, Durham 1847, 4to, 88pp. (D/X 36/5)

**140** *Elizabeth Pease Pease*: W Country 1860, 8vo, 10pp. (D/PE 5/43)

**141** *Edward Backhouse* of Sunderland: Scotland 1869, crown 4to, 56pp. (D/Wa 1/4/7)

**142** *Henry Kitching*: Lancs, Cumb, N Yorks 1877, 4to, 5pp. (D/Ki 347)

**143** *Wilson Pease*: Scotland 1889, 4to, 19pp. (D/GP/55)

**144** *John George Hunter Brown* of Sunderland (1868–1959): Leeds, Glasgow, Manchester, Liverpool 1889–1959, 79 vols, pocket diaries. (D/X 479/1–79)

**145** *Reginald J Mounsey*: Scotland 1905, 4to, 161pp. (D/Wa 3/3/29)

**146** *do*. Scotland, Corn 1909, 4to, 190pp. (D/Wa 3/3/30)

**147** *Helen Mottram* of Darlington: Corn 1909, Shrewsbury 1918, 12mo, 9pp, 6pp. (D/XD 50/2)

## Dyfed

Dyfed Archive Service

Carmarthenshire Record Office, County Hall, Carmarthen, SA31 1JP

**148** *Joseph Gulston*?: Windsor, Oxford, Berkeley Castle 1785, 8vo, 65pp. (Derwydd CA 21)

**149** *Thomas Skeel* of Laugharne: S England, S Wales 1803–1807, 8vo, 110pp. (Museum 304). Published in *The Carmarthenshire Historian*, Vol 8, 1971.

**150** *William Peel* of Taliaris: N Wales 1829, 8vo, 55pp. (Taliaris 313)

**151** *A S Gulston* of Dirleton: Rivers Isis, Severn, Wye, N Wales 1865, 4 vols, 8vo, 22pp, 8pp, 6pp, 20pp. (Derwydd H 26)

Pembrokeshire Record Office, The Castle, Haverfordwest, Dyfed, SA61 2EF

**152** *Anon*: Chester to Milford Haven 1772–1773, 8vo, 27pp. (DDX/81/4)

**153** *Rachel M Allen*: St Albans, Carlisle, Dyfed, Gwent 1877, 8vo, 50pp. (HDX/132/2)

## East Sussex

East Sussex Record Office, The Maltings, Castle Precincts, Lewes, BN7 1YT

**154** *John, later 1st Earl of Ashburnham* (1656–1710): W Suss, Hants, Wilts, Dorset, Devon, Glos, Herefs, Powys, Oxon, Berks 1687, 4to, 55pp. (ASH 933)

**155** *Bertram, 4th Earl of Ashburnham* (1797–1878): Bristol, Glam, Dyfed 1842, 8vo, 64pp. (ASH 974)

**156** *Frances Bridger* (1734–1807): Herts, Beds, Lincs, Hunts, Northants, Yorks, Durham, Derbys, Ches, Lancs, Notts, Cambs, Norf, Suff, Warws 1768, 1772, 8vo, 20pp; Wilts, Dorset, Devon, Corn, Hants 1775; Oxon, Glos, Gwent, Glam, Dyfed 1776, 6pp; Lake District, Scotland 1783, 16pp. (SHR 1928)

**157** *Henry Poole, later 5th Bt (1744–1821):* Surr, Leics, Notts, Yorks, Lancs, Ches, Salop, Powys 1776, 16mo, 11pp. (HOOK 21/2)

**158** *do.* Surr, Hants 1772; Wales, Glos, Som 1770s, 6mo, 7pp. (HOOK 21/3)

**159** *Mary, wife of Sir George Shiffner, 1st Bt (1765–1844):* Oxon, Glos, Gwent, Powys, Som, Dorset, Hants 1790, 6mo, 72pp. (SHR 830A)

**160** *Sir George Shiffner, 1st Bt (1762–1842):* Notts, Yorks, Lake District, Lancs, Derbys 1814; Glos, Gwent 1821, 8vo, 28pp. (SHR 830B)

**161** *George John, 5th Earl de la Warr (1791–1869):* Portsmouth, I of W 1809, 4to, 7pp. (DLW 556)

**162** *Frances Sayer, later Gatty (1803–1875):* Kent, E Suss 1818–1819, 6mo, 36pp, illus. (SAY 3394)

**163** *do.* Kent 1821, 8vo, 32pp, illus. (SAY 3396)

**164** *do.* I of W, Hants 1825, 8vo, 22pp. (SAY 3399)

**165** *do.* I of W, Hants 1826, 6mo 35pp. (SAY 3400)

**166** *do.* N Wales, Salop 1830, 8vo, 23pp. (SAY 3401)

**167** *Frances Gatty (1803–1875):* Lake District, Scotland 1849, 16mo, 70pp. (SAY 3402)

**168** *do.* Lichfield, Chester, Manchester, Liverpool, Lancaster, Carlisle, Scotland 1857, 6mo, 19pp. (SAY 3403)

**169** *Katherine Sayer (1772–1845):* Hants, I of W, Dorset, Som, Devon 1833, 6mo, 17pp. (SAY 3390)

**170** *Charles Henry Gatty (1836–1903):* Hunts, Herts, Lincs, Yorks, Derbys, Kent 1853, 16mo, 31pp. (SAY 3413)

**171** *do.* Kent, Hunts, 1854, 16mo, 24pp. (SAY 3414)

**172** *do.* Norf 1860, 16mo, 5pp. (SAY 3418)

**173** *Charlottle Blencowe (1791–1867):* Derbys, Durham, Northumb, Scotland 1843, 8vo, 26pp. (HOOK 21/6)

**174** *John George Blencowe (1817–1900):* Dorset, I of W 1864, 16mo, 11pp. (HOOK 21/9/10)

**175** *William Grantham (1835–1911):* Chester, Birkenhead, Liverpool 1853; Wales 1853–1854, 8vo, 14pp. (A4789)

**177** *John Douglas Morris (1871–1894):* Oxford 1892, 6mo, 9pp. (AMS 5569/84)

## Essex

Essex Record Office, County Hall, Chelmsford, CM1 1LX

**178** *John Conyers (d.1724):* Cambs, Notts, Yorks, Northumb, Durham, Scotland 1676, 4to, 64pp. (D/DW Z6/1). Extracts published in *Country Life*, 19 Aug 1949.

**179** *Richard Du Cane (1715–1744):* Yorks, Notts, Northants, Beds 1726; Kent 1728–1729, 4to, 100pp. (D/DDc F9)

**180** *William Mildmay (1705–1771):* England, Scotland 1750, 4to, 60pp. (D/DMy, 15M50/1326)

**181** *do.* England, Wales 1751, 4to, 65pp. (D/DMy, 15M50/1325)

**182** *Eliza Bant, Millicent Bant, with Lady Wilson:* Yorks, Notts, Lancs, Lake District 1804; Herts, Notts, Yorks, Scotland 1805, 4to, 90pp. (D/DFr F1)

**183** *Millicent Bant, with Lady Wilson:* Worcs, Herts, Powys, N Wales, Suss 1806; Essex, Cambs, Lincs, Cumb, Scotland 1807, 4to, 71pp. (D/DFr F2)

**184** *do.* Herts, Warws, Cumb, Scotland (incl New Lanark) 1809, 4to, 89pp. (D/DFr F3)

**185** *do.* Som, Glos, Ches, Lancs, Wilts 1813; Bucks, Oxon, Herefs, Powys, S Wales 1808; Great North Road 1809; Herefs, Som, Glos 1812, 3 vols, 4to, 92pp, 10pp, 70pp. (D/DFr F4)

**186** *do.* Wilts, Dorset, Som, Lancs 1813; Som, Ches, Lancs 1814, 4to, 191pp. (D/DFr F5)

**187** *do.* Herts, Bucks, Oxon, Warws 1812, 4to, 121pp. (D/DFr F6)

**188** *do.* Lincs, Yorks, Lancs, Cambs, Scotland, Northumb, Durh m 1816, 4to, 100pp. (D/DFr F7)

**189** *Anon:* Hunts, Leics, Derbys, Yorks, Staffs, Warws, Oxon, Beds, Cambs 1815, 8vo, 40pp. (D/DLu 7/1)

**190** *Caroline Wilkinson of Porchester (Hants):* Hants, Suss, Corn, I of W 1817–1828, 2 vols, 8vo, 44pp. (D/DJg Z23)

**191** *John Round (1783–1860):* Yorks, Lake District, Scotland, Salop 1822, 4to, 31pp. (D/DRh F25/4)

**192** *do.* Wales, Salop 1824, 4to, 30pp. (D/DRh F25/6)

**193** *do.* Kent 1825, 4to, 35pp. (D/DRh F25/7)

**194** *do.* Suss 1826, 4to, 44pp. (D/DRh F25/8)

**195** *Henry Samuel Tabor (1838–1924):* Scotland 1868, 2 vols, 8vo, 18pp, 17pp. (D/DTa F8,9)

**196** *do.* Lake District 1870, 8vo, 114pp. (D/Dta F10)

**197** *do.* N Wales 1872, 1875; S Wales 1873; Devon 1816, 8vo, 150pp. (D/DTa F11)

**198** *do.* Yorks, Scotland 1878, 8vo, 120pp.

(D/DTa F12)

**199** *do.* Lake District 1884; Hants 1887; Devon 1888, N Wales 1889, 8vo, 120pp. (D/DTa F13)

**200** *do.* N Wales 1889; Lincs, Yorks, Durham, Northumb, Cumb, Lake District 1891, 8vo, 100pp. (D/DTa F14)

**201** *do.* Channel Islands, Som 1892; Scotland, Suss 1893; Suss 1894, 8vo, 160pp. (D/DTa F15)

**202** *do.* I of W 1897, 12mo, 46pp. (D/DTa F16)

**203** *do.* Dorset 1895, 8vo, 105pp. (D/DTa F17)

**204** *do.* I of Man, N Wales 1902, 8vo, 120pp. (D/DTa F18)

**205** *do.* Lake District, Corn 1900; Liverpool, Derbys, Suss 1901, 8vo, 70pp. (D/DTa F19)

**206** *do.* Scotland 1904, 8vo, 110pp. (D/Ta F20)

**207** *do.* Yorks 1904, 8vo, 33pp. (D/DTa F21)

**208** *Robert Dawson Poulter*: Essex 1874, 8vo, 22pp. (D/DU 386)

**209** *E A Fitch* (1854–1912): Thames tug 1881, 4to, 17pp. (D/DQs 146/2)

## Glamorgan

Glamorgan Record Office, County Hall, Cathays Park, Cardiff, CF1 3NE

No relevant diaries

## Gloucestershire

Gloucestershire Record Office, Clarence Row, Alvin Street, Gloucester, GL1 3DW

**210** *M de Blainville*: Essex, Cambs, N England 1703, 4to, 60pp. (D1799/F213) Published by Nora Hardwick, *A diary of the journey through the North of England made by William and John Blathwayt of Dyrham Park in 1703*, 1977.

**211** (*Thomas Major*): Norf early 18c, 4to, 68pp. (D421/F32)

**212** *do.* Yorks early 18c, 4to, 8pp. (D421/F32)

**213** *Anon*: S England, Suss, Wilts, Hants 1746, 4to, 8pp. (D421/F18)

**214** *Strickland family*: Yorks, Durham, Scotland 1776, 8vo, 116pp. (D1245/F70)

**215** *George Cumberland*: Glos, Wales 1784, 4to, 57pp. (D225/F38)

**216** *Rev Samuel Viner*: England, Scotland 1781–1801, 15 vols, 8vo, c. 120 pp. (D2227/30)

**217** *Anon* Som, Wales, Herefs, Salop, Derbys, Cumb, Herts 1786, 4to, 36pp. (D421/F18)

**218** *Anon*: Cumb, Lancs, Lake District 1786, 4to, 70pp. (D421/F18)

**219** *Mary Anne Hibbert*: Lake District 1810; I of W, Portsmouth 1812, 4to, 35pp. (D1799/F317)

**220** *do.* Southampton, I of W, Portsmouth 1813, 4to, 15pp. (D1799/F318)

**221** *do.* Bucks, Warws, Staffs, Derbys, Manchester, N Wales, Salop, Oxford 1816, 4to, 80pp. (1799/F320)

**222** *do.* Staffs, Manchester, Brighton 1817, 4to, 15pp. (D1799/F321)

**223** *do.* Som, Glos, Wye Valley, Gwent, Herefs, Salop, Liverpool (music festival), Manchester 1823; York (music festival), N Yorks 1825, 4to, 120pp. (D1799/F322)

**224** *do.* Lancs, Lake District 1829, 8vo, 30pp. (D1799/F324)

**225** *do.* Scotland, Durham, York 1847; Devon, Som 1848, 8vo, 75pp. (D1799/F333)

**226** *do.* N Wales 1849; Scotland 1850, 8vo, 75pp. (D1799/F334)

**227** *do.* Dorset, Devon, Corn 1854; Norwich, Peterborough, Scotland 1855; N Wales 1856; Ely, Lincoln, York, N Yorks 1857; W Wales, Gwent 1858; 8vo, 135pp. (D1799/F337)

**228** *do.* I of W 1859; Yorks, Derbys 1860; Lincs, Leics, Notts, Staffs 1861; Devon 1862; Canterbury, Winchester Cathedrals 1863, 8vo, 75pp. (D1799/F338)

**229** *Sarah Hibbert*: Wilts, Glos, Herefs, Gwent, Welsh Borders 1823, 8vo 30pp. (D1799/F346)

**230** *do.* Lake District 1829, 4to, 15pp. (D1799/F348)

**231** *do.* York Music Festival 1835, 8vo, 20pp. (D1799/F350)

**232** *do.* Devon 1852, 4to, 20pp. (D1799/F352)

**233** *do.* York, Durham, Newcastle upon Tyne, Scotland 1850, 8vo, 90pp. (D1799/F353)

**234** *do.* Dorset, Devon, Corn 1854; Buxton, N Wales 1855, 8vo, 25pp. (D1799/F355)

**235** *do.* Lake District 1853, 12mo, 12pp. (D1799/F357)

**236** *do.* Scotland 1855, 8vo, 50pp. (D1799/F358)

**237** *do.* Yorks 1857, 8vo, 80pp. (D1799/F359)

**238** *do.* I of W 1858; Lake District 1860, 8vo, 20pp, 20pp. (D1799/F360)

**239** *do.* Devon 1862; Canterbury, Manchester, Bournemouth 1863; Norf 1864, 8vo, 20pp, 20pp, 20pp. (D1799/F361)

**240** *Rev W Bushell*: Plynlimon 1829, 8vo, 27pp. (D3616/11)

**241** *Capel family*: Scotland 1838, 8vo, 9pp. (D3393/F13)

**242** *Ellen Letitia Philips*: Lake District 1842, 8vo, 45pp. (D1799/F368)

**243** *Sir William Guise*: Wales 1841, 4to, 64pp. (D326/F46)

**244** *do*. Som, Devon, Corn 1846, 4to, 163pp. (D326/F50)

**245** *do*. Som, Devon 1848, 8vo, 118pp. (D326/F51)

**246** *do*. Lake District 1872, 4to, 122pp. (D326/F53)

**247** *do*. Dorset, Suss, Kent 1878, 12mo, 80pp. (D326/F56)

**248** *do*. Corn, Suss, Surr, Derbys, Northumb, Wales, Scotland c.1860–1880, 7 pocket notebooks, 16mo, each c.120pp. (D326/F57)

**249** *Eliza Coates*: Monmouth, London 1846; Cheltenham 1848, 8vo, 18pp. (D3180/1)

**250** *Anon*: Som, Glos, Wilts 1911, file, 46pp. (D3757/6/1)

**251** *Albert Batty* (1893–1980): diaries or recollections of tours, S England, Wales, Scotland c.1929–1978, 8 vols, 4to. (D3435/1,4,5,48, 49, 51, 52, 54)

## Greater London
Greater London Record Office, 40 Northampton Road, London EC1R 0HB

**252** *Luke Howard*: Yorks, Cumb 1807, 8vo, 82pp. (1017/1397)

## Greater Manchester
Greater Manchester Record Office, 56 Marshall Street, New Cross, Manchester, M4 5FU

No relevant diaries

## Gwent
Gwent Record Office, County Hall, Cwmbran, NP44 2XH

**253** *John Rolls II* (1776–1837): W Glam 1819, 8vo, 119pp. (D361.F/P.3.7)

**254** *do*. W Glam 1820, 8vo, 99pp. (D361.F/P.3.6)

**255** *Elizabeth M Rolls* (b.1813): N Wales, 1844, 8vo, 39pp. (D361.F/P.4.57)

**256** *do*. cruises on *Esmeralda*: Channel Islands, I of W, S Coast 1846–1847, 8vo, 163pp. (D.361.F/P.4.64)

**257** *do*. on *Esmeralda*: Torquay, Falmouth, Scilly Islands, Portsmouth 1849, 8vo, 51pp. (D.361.F/P.4.66)

**258** *do*. on *Camilla*: S Coast 1852, 8vo, 169pp. (D.361.F/P.4.65)

**259** *John A Rolls, Baron Llangattock* (1837–1912): on *Camilla*: S Coast, I of W 1854, 8vo, 14pp. (D.361.F/P.8.107)

**260** *Georgiana Marcia Rolls*: on *Fair Flirt*: Scotland, S Wales, S Coast 1851, 8vo, 198pp. (D.361.F/P.8.112)

## Gwynedd
Gwynedd Archives Service, Caernarfon Record Office, County Offices, Caernarfon, LL55 1SH

**261** *Harriet Alderson*: N Wales 1818, 8vo, 76pp. (XM/2600)

**262** *R M Jackson*: Clwyd 1820, 8vo, 17pp. (XM/6319)

## Hampshire
Hampshire Record Office, 20 Southgate Street, Winchester, SO23 9EF

**263** *Robert Parker* FSA of Maidstone: Wales, Welsh Borders 1804, 4to, 106pp, illus. (18M51/557)

**264** *do*. Glos, Herefs, Salop, Worcs, Wales 1805; Newcastle under Lyne, Liverpool, Caernarfon 1823, 4to, 132pp. (18M51/558)

**265** *Henry Wickham*: Corn, Devon, Som 1807, 8vo, 38pp. (38M49/8/150)

**266** *do*. Yorks, Durham, Northumb, Scotland 1808, 2 vols, 8vo, 38pp, 62pp. (38M49/8/151–152)

**267** *Anon* (Horne or Hutton family): Scotland 1816, 8vo, 139pp. (87M81)

**268** *Rev Thomas Woodhouse* of Ropley: Wales 1865, 4to, 11pp. (8M65/5)

**269** *do*. Hants, I of W, Surr, Warws, Worcs, Welsh Borders 1864, 1884, 4to, 57pp. (8M65/6)

**270** *Laura Elizabeth Palmer*: Yorks, Carlisle, Scotland 1865, 4to, 38pp. (9M68/62)

**271** *do*. Scotland 1871, 8vo, 78pp, illus. (9M68/63)

**272** *Charles Compton Lanchester* of Hannington Rectory, aged 11 years: London 1888, 8vo, 21pp. (149M71/F1)

**273** *Jennie Gauntlett Hill* (1906–1981): Scotland 1925, Wales, W Country 1927, 8vo, 97pp. (130M82/7)

# Hereford and Worcester
Worcester Record Office, County Hall, Spetchley Road, Worcester, WR5 2NP

**274** *Martha Ker, later Porter* of Birlingham: Suss, Hants 1794, 12mo, 13pp. (BA3940/64(i))

**275** *Porter family* of Birlingham: Scotland 1812, 8vo, 7pp. (BA3940/64(i))

**276** *do.* Warws 1814, 16mo, 19pp. (BA3940/63(x))

**277** *do.* Wales 1815, 16mo, 44pp. (BA3940/64(i))

**278** *do.* Scotland 1817–1818, 16mo, 80pp. (BA3940/65(ii))

**279** *Phoebe Porter*: Oxon, Glos, Worcs, Som, Devon, Dorset 1806, 16mo, 15pp. (BA3940/68(i))

**280** *do.* Scotland, Lake District, Yorks, Derbys 1823, 12mo, 44pp. (BA3940/68(i))

**281** *do.* Wye Valley, S Wales 1824; Surr, Kent, Suss, Hants, Wilts, Som, Glos 1825, 8vo, 106pp. (BA3940/68(i))

**282** *Anne Porter*: Scotland, Yorks, Derbys 1823, 12mo, 59pp. (BA3950/65(ii))

**283** *do.* Wye Valley, S Wales 1824, 12mo, 91pp. (BA3490/65(ii))

**284** *do.* Kent, Suss, Hants, Wilts 1825, 12mo, 75pp. (BA3940/29(ii))

**285** *do.* Essex 1842, 1850, 12mo, 45pp. (BA3940/64(i))

**286** *do.* Liverpool, Manchester, Chester, Channel Islands 1846, 12mo, 39pp. (BA3940/64(i))

**287** *do.* Eastern counties 1847, 12mo, 24pp. (BA3940/64(i))

**288** *do.* Lancaster, Lake District, Scotland 1849, 2 vols, 8vo, 63pp, 20pp. (BA3940/66(i))

**289** *do.* Devon, Corn 1858, 16mo, 25pp. (BA3940(i))

**290** *do.* Scotland 1859, 12mo, 32pp, illus. (BA3940/64(i))

**291** *Martha Porter*: Wye Valley, S Wales 1824, 2 vols, 8vo, 80pp, 16pp. (BA3940/64(ii))

**292** *do.* Surr, Kent, Suss 1825, 8vo, 115pp. (BA3490/64(ii))

**293** *John Somerset Russell* (*later Pakington, 1st Baron Hampton*) *of Westwood* (1799–1880): Scotland 1821, 12mo, 60pp. (BA2309/54(x))

**294** *Hannah Williams* of Tenbury Wells: Salop, Wales, Lancs (incl by railroad from Liverpool to Manchester 1831, 8vo, 137pp. (BA9522)

**295** *Hannah A Nott*: Cheltenham 1833; Oxon, Berks, Hants, I of W 1836, 12mo, 23pp. (BA3164/16(iv))

**296** *Nott family*: I of W c.1836, 8vo, 15pp. (BA3264/19)

**297** *do.* Scotland 1850, 8vo, 14pp. (BA3164/19)

**298** *Mrs Manby*: Scotland 1855; London 1893, 8vo, 82pp. (BA3550/2(ii))

**299** *Sladden family*: By steamer from London to Leith; Edinburgh, Glasgow, Scottish Highlands 1859, 4to, 21pp. (BA9520/18(i))

**300** *do.* Yorks 1889, 4to, 6pp. (BA9520(i))

**301** *Sir Julius Sladden* of Badsey (1847–1928): Lake District 1898, 8vo, 43pp. (BA9520/17(vi))

**302** *do.* on *Chieftain* from Oban to Stornoway 1911, 8vo, 12pp. (BA9520/17(vi))

**303** *Anon*: Scotland 1881, 8vo, 38pp. (BA4000/410(i))

**304** *E A B Barnard*: cycle tour of Glos, Som, Devon, Corn; motor tour of N Wales 1904, 4to, 32pp. (BA5828/4(i))

**305** *do.* cycle tour of Salop, N Wales, London, Portsmouth, I of W 1905, 4to, 27pp. (BA5828/4(i))

**306** *do.* Corn, Hants, I of W 1906, 8vo 32pp. (BA5828/4(i))

**307** *Philip Austin Leicester* of Worcester: cycle tour of Cotswolds, Warws, Northants 1911, 8vo, 50pp. (BA8185/2(i))

**308** *do.* cycle tour of Salop, Ches 1912, 8vo, 70pp. (BA8185//2(i))

Hereford Record Office, The Old Barracks, Harold Street, Hereford, HR1 2QX

**309** *Charles Dunne* of Gatley Park: Ludlow to Portsmouth 1807, 8vo, 7pp. (F76/IV/511)

**310** *do.* Swansea to Hereford 1807, 8vo, 7pp. (F76/IV/510)

**311** *Thomas Dunne* of Gatley Park: Ludlow to Edinburgh 1805, 8vo, 5pp. (F76/IV/487)

**312** *do.* Scottish Highlands 1807, 8vo, 35pp. (F76/IV/488)

**313** *John Brydges* of Tyberton: Lond, Kent, Norf 1839, 4to. (K12/99)

## Hertfordshire

Hertfordshire Record Office, County Hall, Hertford, SG13 8DE

**314** *Ralph Radcliffe*: Derbys, Yorks, Durham, Northumb, Scotland 1759, 12mo, 28pp. (D/ER F153)

**315** *James Bucknall Grimston, 3rd Viscount Grimston* (1749–1809): Derbys, Yorks, Warws, Staffs 1768, 2 vols, 12mo, 40pp, 48pp. (D/EV F13–14). Printed in HMC report 1906, pp.229–242.

**316** *do*. Oxon, Som, Wales, Ches, Lancs, Staffs, Warws, Northants 1769, 5 vols, 12mo, 250pp in all. (D/EV F15–19). Printed in HMC report 1906, pp.242–277.

**317** *Mary Martin Leake*: Brighton 1792; Southampton 1794; Norf, Suff 1796; Bath 1798, 8vo, 63pp. (84630)

**318** *William Wilshere*: Dorset, Som 1811, 8vo, 23pp. (61174)

**319** *do*. Suss, Hants, I of W 1811, 8vo, 64pp. (61175)

**320** *do*. Manchester to Liverpool Railway 1833, 12mo, 3pp. (60155)

## Humberside

Humberside Record Office, County Hall, Beverley, HU17 9BA

**321** *Robert D'arcy Hildyard* (d.1814): England, Scotland, Wales 1779–1810, 8 vols, 8vo. each c.75pp. (DD HI)

**322** *Philip Saltmarshe* (1780–1846): Lake District c.1803, 8vo, 21pp. (DD SA 1114)

**323** *Harry Denison* of Waplington (1830–1857): England, Wales 1848–1855, 5 vols, 8vo, 138pp, 192pp, 260pp, 182pp, 156pp. Army service (DD SA 1118–1122)

**324** *Blanche Saltmarshe* (d.1880): Scotland 1852, 4to, 11pp. (DD SA 1116)

**352** *R W Shooter* of Hornsea (1902–1977): England, Scotland 1910–1966, 40 vols, 4to, each c.200pp. (DD SH 1–40)

## Isle of Wight

Isle of Wight Record Office, 26 Hillside, Newport, PO30 3EB

**326** *Anon*: Berks, Hants, Wilts, Suss, Surr, I of W 1776, 12mo, 17pp. (81/98)

**327** *Anthony William Glynn*: Dorset, Devon, Corn, Som 1798, 12mo, 16pp. (OG/TT/71)

**328** *Anon*: Surr, Hants, Suss, I of W 1823, 8vo, 46pp, illus. (IW/98)

**329** *do*. Surr, Hants, I of W 1834, 8vo, 44pp. (IW/98)

**330** *Valentine Beldam*: London, Hants, Suss, I of W 1833, 12mo, 21pp, illus (3). (IW/99)

## Kent

Kent Archives Office, County Hall, Maidstone, ME14 1XQ

**331** *Charles Polhill* (1725–1805): Ripon, London, Bucks, Oxon, Surr, Kent 1764–1781, 8vo, 23pp. (U1007 F1)

**332** *George Polhill* (1767–1839): Hants, Suss 1789–1790, 8vo, 11pp. (U1007 F2)

**333** *Sir Joseph Banks* (1743–1820): S Coast, Irish Sea, Hebrides 1772, crown 4to, 110pp. (U1590 S1/2)

**334** *Thomas Baskerfield*: Kent, Suss, Surr 1792, crown 4to, 45pp, illus. (U2668 F1)

**335** *Edward Hussey senr*?: Lake District early 19c, 12mo, 27pp. (U1776 F6)

**336** *Anon*: Hastings 1805, 8vo, 40pp. (U1272 F2)

**337** *Anon*: Kent 1809, fo, 16pp. (U2402 F1). Published: ed. J Whyman, 'The Kentish Portion of an Anonymous Tour of 1809' in *Studies in Modern Kentish History*, ed. A P Detsicas and W N Yates, Kent Archaeological Society, Maidstone 1983, pp. 139–186.

**338** *Mary Ann Coare*: Hants 1810, 8vo, 25pp. (U1823/8 Z1)

**339** *do*. Maidstone to Canterbury and back 1812, 8vo, 40pp. (U1823/8 Z2)

**340** *do*. Kent, Suss, Hants, I of W 1829, 8vo, 19pp. (U1823/8 Z3)

**341** *do*. W Midlands, Wales c.1830, 8vo, 45pp. (U1823/8 Z4)

**342** *William Bland* of Hartlip: Ireland via Oxford 1808, 8vo, 37pp, illus. (U771 F3)

**343** *do*. Scotland 1812, 34pp. (U771 F5)

**344** *do*. Cambs, Norf 1839, 16mo, 40pp. (U771 F8)

**345** *do*. Wales, W Midlands 1839, 4 vols, 8vo, 85pp, illus. (U771 F13)

**346** *do*. Berks, Som, Glos 1842, 16mo, 23pp. (U771 F12)

**347** *do*. Essex, Suff, Norf 1843, 16mo, 35pp.

(U771 F12)

**348** *do.* London, Derbys, Yorks, Durham, Newcastle upon Tyne, Lake District c.1850, 8vo, 40pp. (U771 F11)

**349** *do.* W Country, W Midlands, Bangor, Lichfield 1851, 16mo, 153pp. (U771 F14)

**350** *do.* Yorks, Lancs, Lake District 1854, 16mo, 116pp. (U771 F15)

**351** *do.* Scotland 1861, 16mo, 131pp. (U771 F18)

**352** *Anon*: Yorks, Durham 1814, 8vo, 19pp. (U1127 F14)

**353** *F C Amherst* (1807–1829): Cheltenham 1819, 8vo, 26pp., illus. (U1350 F2)

**354** *do.* Worcs, Warws 1821, 8vo, 31pp., illus. (U1350 F3)

**355** *do.* Salop 1822, 8vo, 43pp., illus. (U1350 F4)

**356** *Charles Powell* of Speldhurst: Kent 1832, 8vo, 19pp. (U934 F8). Published: ed. F Hull, 'A Kentish Holiday, 1823', *Archaeologia Cantiana*, lxxxi (1966), pp. 109–117.

**357** *Lucy Papillon?*: Northants 1836, 8vo, 8pp. (U1015 F86/5)

**358** *L S Daniele*: Kent 1844, 8vo, 160pp., illus. (U2666 F1)

**359** *Emily, Countess Stanhope* (d.1873): Lake District, Scotland 1846, 1849, 4to, 50pp., illus. (U1590 C478/3)

**360** *J G Talbot MP* (1835–1910): N England, Scotland 1846; S Wales 1847; Suss 1848; Yorks 1849, 8vo, 52pp. (U1612 F48)

**361** *do.* Yorks 1849; Devon, Corn 1850; N Wales 1852, 8vo, 35pp. (U1612 F49)

**362** *Mrs E M Wood* (1893–1966): Channel Islands c.1920, 8vo, 19pp. (U1390 F56)

**353** *do.* Tenterden 1923, 8vo, 55pp. (U1390 F57)

## Lancashire
Lancashire Record Office, Bow Lane, Preston, PR1 8ND

**364** *William Cross*: N Wales, Liverpool, Chester, Salop 1790, 8vo, 49pp. (DDX 841/3/1)

**365** *Anon*: Lancs to London, Cambs, Home Counties c.1808, 4to, 33pp. (DDB 64/14)

**366** *Anon*: Hants 1812, 4to, 121pp. (DDX 274/9)

**367** *Anon*: Scotland 1819, 4to, 24pp. (DDX 274/12)

**368** *Richard Hodgkinson*: Lancs, Lincs (Crowland) 1822, 8vo, 33pp. (DDX 211/33)

**369** *Mrs Greene Bradley* of Slyne House: Chester, N Wales 1830–1831, 8vo, 44pp. (DDGr F1)

**370** *Anon*: Lake District, Wales, Wye Valley, Glos 1844, 8vo, 102pp., illus. (DDX 1282/4)

## Leicestershire
Leicestershire Record House, 57 New Walk, Leicester, LE1 7JB

**371** *Anon*: Scotland 1793, 8vo, 67pp. (DE 546)

**372** *Eliza Spurrett*: Staffs, Salop, N Wales 1825, 8vo, 77pp. (7D54/2/1)

**373** *do.* London 1827, 8vo, 67pp. (7D54/2/2)

**374** *do.* London, Ramsgate 1839; N Wales 1841; Derbys 1842; Clifton, Wye Valley 1844, 8vo, 75pp. (7D54/2/3)

**375** *do.* I of W, Leamington 1845; Stratford, London 1846; Cheltenham 1847; Brighton 1849; London, Ramsgate 1851; 8vo, 95pp. (7D54/2/4)

**376** *Rev Robert Martin*: Wales, I of Man, Scotland, Derbys, I of W, Channel Islands 1829–1834, 8vo, 67pp. (DG 6/C/13)

**377** *Thomas Condon*: Leics 1869–1870, 12mo, 49pp. (DE 2337/4)

## Lincolnshire
Lincolnshire Archives Office, The Castle, Lincoln, LN1 3AB

**378** *Thomas Worsley*: England 1750, 8vo, c.83pp. (Worsley 37)

**379** *Mrs William Monson*: N England, Scotland, London 1793, 8vo, 63pp. (MON 15/C/1)

**380** *S Metcalfe*: same tour as 379, 8vo, c.80pp. (MON 15/C/2)

**381** *William Monson*: Oxon, Warws, Lake District, Lancs 1816, 1 vol. (MON 15/B/2)

**382** *do.* Yorks, Durham, Scotland, early 19c, 1 vol. (MON 15/B/13)

**383** *do.* Lake District, Salop, Worcs, Derbys, Glos early 19c, 1 vol. (MON 15/B/14)

**384** *Jonathan Field*: Wales 1805, 8vo, 5pp. (Field 2/5/4)

**385** *Harriet Mundy*: Plymouth, W Country 1819, 1 vol. (MM 10/32)

**386** *Francis Augustus Fane*: England, Scotland 1849–1884, 24 vols, 8vo. (Fane 6/8/1/2,4,6–10, 12, 14–19, 23, 26–30, 33, 34, 36, 37)

**387** *G K Jarvis*: England 1852, 4to, c.26pp. (Jarvis VI/C/4)

**388** *Edmund Royds*: England, Scotland 1925–1933, 4to, c.150pp. (Fane 6/12/6/A–F)

# Norfolk
Norfolk Record Office, Central Library, Norwich, NR2 1NJ

**389** *Hamon L'Estrange*: Lincs, Yorks, Durham, Northumb, Scotland, Ches, Notts, Hunts, Oxon, Northants 1713, 8vo, 24pp. (NF 2)

**390** *Charles Perry*: Northants, Lincs, Notts, Yorks, Lancs, Derbys, Leics, Oxon, Som, Wilts 1725, 8vo, 70pp. (MC 150/49 625 x 3)

**391** *James Coldham*: Northumb, Yorks 1752; Kent 1753, 12mo, 44pp. (MC 40/101 485 x 9)

**392** *do*. Northants, Leics, Notts, Derbys, Ches, Yorks, Lancs 1767, 12mo, 46pp. (MC 40/103 485 x 9)

**393** *Rev John Price*: Norf, Suff 1757, 8vo, 25pp. (Colman 174)

**394** *Thomas de Grey*: Wales 1769, 4to, 188pp. (WLS LXX/2 481 x 6)

**395** *Robert Triphook*: Surr, Hants, I of W, Wilts, Windsor 1805, 4to, 148pp. (DS 622 P 137 C)

**396** *Mr Marten*: Norf 1825, 8vo, 150pp, illus. (MC 26/1 504 x)

**397** *Anon*: Norf, London, Bath, Windsor 1826–1838, 8vo, 180pp. (MS80 T 131 C)

**398** *John Bilby*: Peterborough, Lincoln, Newark, Nottingham 1828, 8vo, 62pp. (MC 27/2 501 x 4)

**399** *Rev Thomas and Mrs Howes*: Cheltenham 1828, 16mo, 40pp. (MC 150/56 625 x 4)

**400** *Mary Anne Lee Warner*: Yorks, Derbys 1828, 4to, 6pp. (BUL 7/20 615 x 1)

**401** *Rev Thomas Starling Buckle?*: Norf, Cambs, Lincs, Yorks, Durham, Northumb, Scotland 1841?, 12mo, 38pp. (WKC 6/377 403 x 8)

**402** *George C Eaton*: Derbys, Warws, Oxon, London, Kent, Suss 1848, 4to, 108pp. (Eaton 4.2.71 II)

**403** *do*. Lake District, Scotland 1849, 4to, 108pp. (Eaton 4.2.71 III)

**404** *do*. Hants, I of W, Wilts 1850, 4to, 108pp. (Eaton 4.2.71 IV)

**405** *do*. Devon, Corn 1851, 4to, 108pp. (Eaton 4.2.71 V)

**406** *do*. Scotland 1852, 4to, 104pp. (Eaton 4.2.71 VII)

**407** *do*. Snowdonia 1863, 8vo, 16pp. (Eaton 4.2.71 VII)

**408** *do*. London, I of W 1872, crown 4to, 20pp. (Eaton 4.2.71 VII)

**409** *do*. Scotland 1873, 4to, 108pp. (Eaton 4.2.71 VII)

**410** *do*. I of W 1876, 4to, 76pp. (Eaton 4.2.71 VII)

**411** *do*. Lake District 1877, crown 4to, 130pp. (Eaton 4.2.71 VII)

**412** *do*. N Wales 1879, 4to, 104pp. (Eaton 4.2.71 VII)

**413** *do*. Walton on the Naze 1880, 4to, 28pp. (Eaton 4.2.71 VII)

**414** *do*. Whitby 1883, 4to, 50pp. (Eaton 4.2.71 VII)

**415** *do*. London, Wales, Suff 1886, crown 4to, 78pp. (Eaton 4.2.71 VII)

**416** *do*. Scotland 1887, 4to, 108pp. (Eaton 4.2.71 VII)

**417** *do*. N Wales 1888, crown 4to, 84pp. (Eaton 4.2.71 VII)

**418** *do*. Bournemouth 1892, crown 4to, 40pp. (Eaton 4.2.71 VII)

**419** *do*. London, Scotland 1895, 4to, 64pp. (Eaton 4.2.71 VII)

**420** *Partridge family*: Norf 1863–1869, 8vo, 98pp. (MC 55/77 506 x 5)

**421** *Henry James Coldham*: Rosshire 1864, 12mo, 62pp. (MC 40/222 486 x 5)

**422** *do*. Scotland c.1868, 8vo, 16pp. (MC 40/239 386 x 6)

**423** *Rev James Lee Warner*: Glos, Oxon, Salop, Wales 1883; Warws, Yorks, Cumb, Scotland, Northumb 1886, 8vo, 50pp. (Lee Warner 18/3 441 x 4)

**424** *Dorothy Kingsbury*: London, Suff, Norf, Devon, Scotland, c.1883–1904, 4to, 119pp. (MC 29 468 x)

**425** *Caroline Tomkins*: Norf 1885–1887, 12mo, 44pp. (MC 81/16 525 x 7)

**426** *Harriet and Henry John Copeman*: N Devon 1886, 4to, 70pp. (MC 81/17 525 x 7)

**427** *E A Field*: Scotland 1914, 4to, 100pp. (MC 57/37 507 x 4)

**428** *do*. Wales 1915, 4to, 101pp. (MC 57/39 507 x 4)

**429** *do*. Glos, Som, Devon, Corn, Wilts 1919, 4to, 66pp. (MC 57/40 507 x 4)

**430** *do*. Derbys, Salop, Herefs 1920, 4to, 61pp. (MC 57/41 507 x 4)

**431** *do*. Yorks 1921, 4to, 16pp. (MC 57/42 507 x 4)

**432** *G L Harrison*: Norf 1918–1919, 8vo, 23pp. (Gulley 3.8.85)

## North Yorkshire
North Yorkshire Record Office, County Hall, Northallerton, DL7 8AD

**433** *William Gray senr (1751–1845)*: Scotland 1796, 2 vols, 56pp, 28pp. (ZGY/T1,1b)

**434** *do*. York to Bath, Derbys 1809–1811, 1 vol, 42pp. (ZGY/T5)

**435** *do*. Yorks 1806–1816, 1 vol, 20pp. (ZGY/T10)

**436** *Jonathan Gray (1779–1837)*: Scotland 1796, 3 vols, 60pp, 112pp, 45pp. (ZGY/T2a–c)

**437** *do*. N Wales 1796, 2 vols, 56pp, 62pp, illus (36). (ZGY/T3a–c)

**438** *do*. West Country, S Wales 1802, 1 vol, 108pp, illus. (ZGY/T4)

**439** *Margaret Gray (1809–1826)*: I of Man 1822, 1 vol, 48pp. (ZGY/T7)

**440** *do*. N Yorks 1823; London, Cambridge 1825, 1 vol, 66pp. (ZGY/T8)

## Northamptonshire
Northamptonshire Record Office, Delapre Abbey, Northampton NN4 9AW

**441** *Sir Justinian Isham* of Lamport (1687–1737): Bath 1730, 12mo, 74pp. (I.L. 2688)

**442** *Robert Andrew* of Harlestone (d.1807): Oxon, Glos, Powys, Glam, Som, Devon, Dorset, Wilts, Hants, Berks 1752, 8vo, 65pp. (Andrew 280)

**443** *Rev Stotherd Abdy* (d.1773): Berks 1770, 8vo, 68pp. (Fitzwilliam (Milton) Misc. Vol.2)

**444** *John Thornton* of Brockhall (1800–1851): I of W 1817, 8vo, 51pp. (Th 3181)

**445** *do*. Warws, Worcs, Staffs (Coalbrookdale) 1819, 4to, 18pp. (Th 3182)

**446** *do*. Norf 1821, 2 vols, 8vo, 36pp, 20pp. (Th 3183, 3184)

**447** *do*. Wales 1823, 8vo, 40pp. (Th 3186)

**448** *do*. Devon 1824, 8vo, 5pp. (Th 3187)

**449** *Hon Barbara Cockayne Medlycott* of Rushton (1753–1838): Bristol 1819; Kent, Yorks 1824, sq 8vo, 37pp. (C.1472)

**450** *Booth family* of Glendon: Lancs, Yorks 1834, crown 4to, 8pp. (Gompertz (Glendon) 177)

## Northumberland
Northumberland Record Office, Melton Park, North Gosforth, Newcastle upon Tyne, NE3 5QX

**451** *George Culley (1735–1813)*: Leics, Midlands, S England, London, Yorks 1765, 4to, 35pp. (ZCU.1/1)

**452** *do*. Yorks, Leics, Midlands, Cambs, Lincs, Scottish Lowlands 1771, 8vo, 30pp. (ZCU.1/3)

**453** *Matthew Culley (1731–1804)*: Scottish Lowlands, Aberdeen 1770, 4to, 31pp. (ZCU.1/2)

**454** *do*. Scottish Lowlands, Cumb 1794, 12mo, 60pp. (ZCU.1/4)

**455** *do*. Durham, Yorks, Notts, Leics 1798, 8vo, 30pp. (ZCU.1/5)

**456** *Sir Edward Blackett Bt (1719–1804)*: Lake District, Solway Moss inundation 1792, 4to, 28pp. (ZBL.243)

**457** *Edward Blackett (1752–1796)*: Lake District, Solway Moss inundation 1792, 4to, 13pp. (ZBL.243)

**458** *T J Parke and B Parke*: N Wales 1813, 8vo, 100pp. (ZRI.31/2/7)

**459** *Sir M W Ridley Bt (1778–1836)*: Worcs, Glos, Som, Wye Valley 1814, 8vo, 50pp. (ZRI.32/3/8)

**460** *do*. Scotland (incl New Lanark) 1824, 8vo, 20pp. (ZRI.32/3/16)

**461** *Sir Charles Monck Bt (1779–1867)*: Northumb, Durham, Yorks, Derbys 1825–1826, 12mo, 50pp. (ZMI/B33/XXXVII)

**462** *Anon*: Edinburgh 1831, 12mo, 30pp. (ZMI/B33/XXXVIII)

## Nottinghamshire
Nottinghamshire Archives Office, County House, High Pavement, Nottingham, NG1 1HR

**463** *Anon*: Scotland, Carlisle, Liverpool, Manchester, Nottingham c.1764, 8vo, 140pp. (M 380)

**464** *Abigail Gawthern*: London 1802; Bath, Bristol, Weymouth 1805, fo, 24pp. (M 23,904). Published: ed. A Henstock, *The Diary of Abigail Gawthern of Nottingham 1751–1810*, Thoroton Society Record Series, 33, 1980.

**465** *Henry Porter Lowe (later Sherbrooke) and*

*Robert Lowe*: Barmouth 1831; Lake District, Glasgow, Scotland 1833, 4to, 200pp. (DD.SK 218/1)

**466** *do*. Paignton 1832, 2 vols, 8vo, 92pp, 44pp. (DD.SK 219/2/1–2)

**467** *Anon*: Nottingham, Manchester, Liverpool, Bangor, Worcester, Birmingham 1834, 8vo, 24pp. (DD. 109/1)

**468** *'J E B'*: Notts (places associated with Lord Byron) 1870, 4to, 82pp, illus. (M 481)

**469** *Margaret Alice Byron*: Essex, London, Surr, Suss, Hants, Leics, Notts, Derbys, Staffs, Yorks, Cumb, Scotland, N Wales 1886–1887, 1890–1893, 3 vols, 8vo, each 120pp. (DD 704/1–3)

# Oxfordshire

Oxfordshire Record Office, County Hall, Oxford, OX1 1ND

**470** *Lord Quarendon, later 3rd Earl of Litchfield*: N England (incl York, Doncaster), Leics, Bucks 1754, 8vo, 7pp. (DIL.XX/a/7a)

**471** *do*. Hants, I of W 1755, 4to, 3pp. (DIL.XX/a/7a)

**472** *William Francis Lowndes Stone*: Surr, Hants, Wilts, Glos, Herefs, Gwent, Powys 1834, 4to, 21pp. (LSN.VII/i/l)

**473** *Oliver Aplin?*: Devon, W Country 1886; Norf 1888, 12mo, 38pp. (Apl.III/iii/2)

**474** *G A F Budd*: Kent, London 1919, fo, 4pp. (Misc.Budd.XIII/3)

**475** *do*. Oxon 1921, fo, 4pp. (Misc.Budd.XIII/4)

# Powys

Powys Archives Service, County Library Headquarters, Cefnllys Road, Llandrindod Wells, LD1 5LD

No relevant diaries

# Shropshire

Shropshire Record Office, The Shire Hall, Abbey Foregate, Shrewsbury, SY2 6ND

**476** *Robert Flint, later Corbett* of Micklewood and Longnor: Salop, Herefs, Powys 1754, 8vo, 14pp. (567/5/3/1/43)

**477** *do*. Staffs, Derbys, Notts, Yorks 1757; Yorks 1789, crown 8vo, 58pp. (567/5/3/1/44)

**478** *Anon*: Bucks, London, Essex, Kent, Cambs, Hunts, Northants 1775, 8vo, 61pp. (2118/227)

**479** *S Butler*: Birmingham 1781; Salop 1782, 16mo, 98pp. (2495/Box 16)

**480** *Katherine Plymley* of Longnor: Salop 1794, 8vo, 48pp. (1066/27)

**481** *do*. Herefs, Salop 1795, 8vo, 48pp. (1066/33)

**482** *do*. Clwyd, Gwynedd, Anglesey 1792, 3 vols, 8vo, 48pp, 44pp, 44pp. (567/5/5/1/1–3)

**483** *do*. Glos, Som 1794, 2 vols, 8vo, each 40pp. (567/5/5/1/4–5)

**484** *do*. Oxford, London, Bath 1795, 2 vols, 8vo, each 40pp. (567/5/5/1/6–7)

**485** *do*. Salop, Birmingham, Warws, Oxford, Oxon, Berks, London 1796, 7 vols, 8vo, 40–48pp. (567/5/5/1/8–14)

**486** *do*. Glos, Bath 1796, 2 vols, 8vo, 44, 48pp. (567/5/5/1/15–16)

**487** *do*. Salop, Worcester, Bath 1799, 8vo, 44pp. (567/5/5/1/17)

**488** *do*. Oxford, Oxon, Worcester 1801, 2 vols, 8vo, 58, 52pp. (567/5/5/1/18–19)

**489** *do*. Salop, Powys, Herefs, Dyfed, Corn 1802–1803, 7 vols, 8vo, 88–100pp. (567/5/5/1/20–26)

**490** *do*. Bath 1807, 8vo, 92pp. (567/5/5/1/27)

**491** *do*. Staffs, Leics, Northants, Beds, Herts, London, Oxford, Stratford on Avon 1813, 8vo, 92pp. (567/5/5/1/28)

**492** *do*. Oxford, London, Warws, Ches, Clwyd, Powys 1814, 2 vols, 8vo, 94, 96pp. (567/5/5/1/29–30)

**493** *do*. Staffs, Birmingham, Warws, Northants, Beds, Herts, London, Kent, Suss, Essex, Cambridge, Hunts, Leics 1814, 2 vols, 8vo, 96, 92pp. (567/5/5/1/31–32)

**494** *Anon*: Clwyd, Powys, Salop c.1812, 4to, 4pp. (2089/9/5/59)

**495** *Louisa Charlotte Kenyon*: Clwyd, Gwynedd, Salop 1803, 8vo, 90pp, illus. (549/212)

**496** *do*. Gwent, Glam, W Glam, Dyfed 1837, 12mo, 68pp, illus. (549/285)

**497** *do*. Clwyd, Gwynedd 1839, 12mo, 127pp, illus. (549/286)

**498** *do*. Salop, Worcs, Glos, Wilts, Som, Herefs 1844, 12mo, 156pp, illus. (549/288)

**499** *do*. Derbys, Notts, Staffs, Ches, Salop, Clwyd c.1847, 24mo, 93pp, illus. (549/291)

**500** *do.* Salop, Worcs, Derbys, Herefs, Glos, 1848, 12mo, 16pp, illus. (549/288)

**501** *T B Ebrall*: Aberystwyth 1866; I of Man 1867; Liverpool 1868, 8vo, 160pp. (3971)

## Somerset
Somerset Record Office, Obridge Road, Taunton, TA2 7PU

**502** *John Walker* (d.c.1711): London to E Anglia 1672; to Scotland 1674; to Wales 1676; Channel Islands 1677; Northampton to Derbys, Lincoln, Kent 1677–1682, 1 vol, fo, 8pp, 27pp, 20pp, 10pp, 15pp. (DD/WHb 3087)

**503** *Caleb Dickinson* of Kingweston (d.1783): Bristol to Liverpool, Manchester, York 1740, 8vo, 41pp. (DD/DN 230)

**504** *William Dickinson?*: Som, Devon, Corn 1776, 8vo, 40pp. (DD/DN 486)

**505** *Thomas Carew* of Crowcombe Court (1702–1766)?: London, Kent c.1744, 4to, 25pp. (DD/TB 18/4)

**506** *Anon* (companion of Thomas Carew?): London, Kent, E Anglia 1744, 4to, 10pp, 16pp. (DD/TB 14/25)

**507** *Rev John Skinner* (d.1839): Som, Devon, Corn 1797; Som, Devon, S Coast to Kent 1801; Northumb (Roman Wall) 1801; Lake District 1801, 1 vol, 8vo, 123pp, 81pp, 88pp, 90pp. (DD/SAS C/1193/10)

**508** *W Spurle* of Taunton: Taunton to York 1802; Som, Glos 1803, 1 vol, small 4to, 203pp, 62pp. (DD/X/HC/1)

**509** *E J Esdaile* of Cothelstone (1785–1867): Som, Devon 1810, small 4to, 100pp. (DD/ES Box 14)

**510** *do.* Lake District, Devon 1823, 4to, 83pp. (DD/ES Box 17)

**511** *Eland Clatworthy* of Taunton: Scotland 1883, 8vo, 35pp. (DD/CT 66)

## South Yorkshire
Barnsley Archive Service, Central Library, Shambles Street, Barnsley, S70 2JF

No relevant diaries

Doncaster Archives Department, King Edward Road, Balby, Doncaster, DN4 0NA

**512** *Isabella Aldam*: Lake District 1831, 8vo, 22pp. (DD.WA)

**513** *do.* Lake District 1832, 8vo, 15pp. (DD/WA)

**514** *William Aldam*: Yorks, Staffs, Worcs, Devon, Corn 1833, 8vo, 27pp. (DD/WA)

**515** *do.* Cambridge, London, Suss 1834, 8vo, 31pp. (DD./WA)

**516** *do.* Scotland 1838, 8vo, 24pp. (DD/WA)

**517** *do.* London, Channel Islands 1840, 8vo, 34pp. (DD/WA)

Rotherham Metropolitan Borough, Brian O'Malley Central Library, Walker Place, Rotherham, S65 1JH

**518** *Richard Holden* (1768–1809): Yorks, Lancs, Lake District 1808, 4to, 11pp. (2/F1/1). Extracts published in *Manchester Guardian*, September 1953.

Sheffield Record Office, Central Library, Surrey Street, Sheffield, S1 1XZ

No relevant diaries

## Staffordshire
Staffordshire Record Office, County Buildings, Eastgate Street, Stafford, ST16 2LZ

**519** *Hon Henry Legge* (1765–1844): N England 1787, 2 vols, 4to, 67pp, 8vo, 21pp. (D(W) 1778/V/1110)

**520** *Charles Jerningham*: N England, Midlands 1797, 8vo, 26pp. (D641/3/P/4/11/7)

**521** *Thomas Twemlow* of Betley (1782–1872): I of W, Hants 1806, 8vo, 9pp. (D952/3/2/4)

**522** *Harriet Frances Congreve*: London 1826, 4to, 23pp. (D1057/P/4)

## Suffolk
Suffolk Record Office, St Andrew House, County Hall, Ipswich, IP4 2JS

**523** *William Kirby senr.* (1719–1791): Bath 1756; Cambs, Northants 1759, 8vo, 22pp. (HA21/B1/1)

**524** *Rev William Kirby junr.* (1759–1850): Cambs 1803, 1804, 1808, 8vo, 49pp. (HA/21/C1/1)

**525** *Eliza Pretyman*: Lincs, Yorks 1794, 4to, 58pp. (HA119:T108/26)

**526** —*Blois*: N Wales 1795, 8vo, 44pp. (HA30:50/22/6.1(1))

**527** —*Betts-Doughty*: Wales 1816, 3 vols, 8vo, 36pp, 21pp, 9pp. (HD79/AF2/3/1–3)

**528** *Gathorne Gathorne-Hardy, 1st Earl of Cranbrook* (aged 13): Scotland 1827, 8vo, 36pp. (HA43:T501/149)

**529** *Harriet Walker*: Suff, London, Scotland 1837, 8vo, 40pp. (HD236/3/5)

**530** *Elizabeth Sarah White*: Suss 1849; Oxford 1852, 8vo, c.200pp. (HA244/K/25)

**531** *do*. Devon (Lynmouth) 1881, 8vo, 80pp. (HA244/K/14)

**532** *do*. Oxford 1886, 8vo, 20pp. (HA244/K/17)

**533** *do*. Derbys 1887, 8vo, 9pp. (fragment) (HA244/K/19)

**534** *White family*: Cumb 1886, 8vo, (HA244/K/18)

**535** *do*. Devon 1889, 8vo, (HA244/K/21)

**536** *do*. Corn 1890, 8vo, (HA244/K/24)

**537** *Hon Agnes Eden*: Scotland 1888, 1899, 8vo, 64pp, illus. (HA58/2/1)

Bury St Edmunds Branch Office, Raingate Street, Bury St Edmunds, IP33 1RX

**538** *Rev Sir John Cullum*: England, Wales 1767–1775, 7 vols, 8vo, 365pp, 351pp, 351pp, 347pp, 219pp, 150pp, 60pp., 2 vols illus. (E2/44/1–5)

**539** *Sir John Cullum*: W Country 1779, 8vo, 87pp, illus. (E2/33/2)

**540** *Sir Thomas Gery Cullum*: Devon 1789, 8vo, 75pp. (E2/44/6)

**541** *Rev Sir Thomas Gery Cullum and Sir William Gell*: Scotland 1799–1800, 8vo, c.123pp. (E2/42/6)

**542** *Rev Sir Thomas Gery Cullum*: Scotland 1810–1811, 4 vols, 8vo, 60pp, 35pp, 60pp, 40pp. (E2/44/48–51)

**543** *Susanna Cullum*: England 1799–1801, 6 vols, 8vo, 26pp, 5pp, 22pp, 6pp, 74pp, 30pp. (E2/44/62–67)

**544** *Anne Cullum*: England 1835–1838, 8vo, 43pp. (E2/44/60)

**545** *Gen William Hervey*: Scotland 1767; Wales 1768–1770; England 1770–1800, 33 vols, 8vo, each c.80pp, illus. (941/53/5–9)

**546** *J Mason*: N England 1779; W Country 1780, 8vo, 218pp. (E2/42/5)

**547** *Rev E M Farrer*: Suff, Norf 1905–1929, 36 vols, 8vo, each c.70–80pp, illus. (2186/1–36)

Lowestoft Branch Office, Central Library, Clapham Road, Lowestoft, NR32 1DR

**548** *Lady Pleasance Smith*: London 1804, 8vo, 50pp. (12/1)

**549** *John Barber Scott*: Suff, London 1806, 8vo, 7pp. (185/1/1)

**550** *do*. England, Scotland 1831–1832, 8vo, 120pp. (185/1/14)

**551** *do*. Wales, W Country 1838, 8vo, 120pp. (185/1/21)

**552** *do*. Wales, W Country 1842, 8vo, 120pp. (185/1/32)

**553** *do*. W Country 1843–1844, 8vo, 120pp. (185/1/36)

**554** *do*. Channel Islands 1845, 8vo, 120pp. (185/1/41)

**555** *do*. I of W 1846, 8vo, 120pp. (185/1/44)

**556** *do*. I of Man, England, Wales 1848, 8vo, 120pp. (185/1/48)

**557** *do*. I of W 1858–1859, 8vo, 120pp. (185/1/72) Extracts from Scott's diaries have been published: Ethel Mann, *An Englishman at Home & Abroad*, London, 1930.

**558** *Samuel Scott*: Oxon, Glos, Som 1821, 3 vols, 8vo, each 44pp. (185/2/3–6)

## Surrey
Surrey Record Office, County Hall, Kingston-upon-Thames, KT1 2DN

**559** *Maria Frances Wyatt Edgell* (d.1879): N Wales, Lake District, S W Scotland 1857, 12mo, 52pp. (2088/8)

**560** *James Chuter Ede* (1882–1965): cycle rides, Surr, Kent 1905, 8vo, 42pp. (390/11/15)

**561** *do*. N Scotland 1948, 8vo, 124pp. (390/11/18)

**562** *do*. N Scotland 1949, 8vo, 64pp. (390/11/19)

**563** *Leslie Todd*: mainly weekend cycle rides and walks in S E England and annual holidays: 1924; 1925; Whitby 1929; Corn 1930; Yorks 1931; E Anglia 1932; Salop, Mid-Wales 1933; E Anglia 1934; E Anglia 1935; Yorks 1936; 1937; Devon, Corn 1938; 1939; Devon 1940–1; Devon 1941–2; Bournemouth 1942–3; Devon 1943–4; Devon, Salop 1944–6; Devon 1946–8; Suff 1948–9; Lake District 1949–51; Suff 1951–2; Devon

1952–3; Suff, I of W 1953–4; Dorset 1954–5; Suff 1956–7; Suss, N Wales 1957–9; Suff 1959–63; Lake District 1963–7, 29 vols, 8vo and 12mo, 103pp, 144pp, or 183pp. (2830/1/3–32)

Guildford Muniment Room, Castle Arch, Guildford, GU1 3SX

**564**  *William Bray* (1736–1832): England, Wales, Scotland 1756–1818, fo, c.800pp. (85/2/5)

# Tyne and Wear
Tyne and Wear Archives Sevice, Blandford House, Blandford Square, Newcastle upon Tyne, NE1 4JA

**565**  *William Dunn* of Newcastle: Lake District, London, Manchester 1887, 8vo, 157pp. (T.W.A.S. 996/1)

# Warwickshire
Warwickshire Record Office, Priory Park, Cape Road, Warwick, CV34 4JS

**566**  *Sophia, Lady Newdigate*: Bucks, Berks, Herts, Essex, Surr, Suss, I of W, Hants, Wilts, Som, Glos 1747, crown 4to, 56pp, illus. (CR.1841/7)

**567**  *do*. Leics, Derbys, Notts mid-1750s, crown 4to, 20pp, illus. (CR.1841/7)

**568**  *Sir Roger Newdigate*: Notts, Yorks, Durham, Northumb, Edinburgh, Dunkeld, return via W Coast to Penrith 1766, 8vo, 64pp. (CR.136/A563)

**569**  *Anon*: Malvern down R Severn into S Wales 18 c, 8vo, 26pp. (CR.136/A48)

**570**  *Francis Newdigate*: Derbys 1833, 12mo, 54pp. (CR.136/A271)

**571**  *do*. Kent 1835, 8vo, 30pp. (CR.136/A273)

**572**  *do*. N Yorks 1836, 8vo, 78pp. (CR.136/A274)

**573**  *do*. Kent 1837, 8vo, 54pp. (CR.136/A280)

**574**  *do*. Kent, Berks, Surr 1838, 8vo, 32pp. (CR.136/A276)

**575**  *do*. Kent 1838, 8vo, 34pp. (CR.136/A277)

**576**  *do*. Kent, S Coast 1839, 12mo, 56pp. (CR.136/A278)

**577**  *do*. W Country, Kent, N England 1844, 12mo, 24pp. (CR.136/A282)

**578**  *do*. Derbys 1840, 1847; Som 1842; Staffs 1847, 12mo, 50pp. (CR.136/A275)

**579**  *Charles Newdigate*: Worcs, Clwyd, Staffs 1840, 8vo, 34pp. (CR.136/A279)

**580**  *Rev C J Newdigate*: N Wales 1868, 8vo, 140pp. (CR.136/A285)

**581**  *Anon*: Hants, Kent, Surr, Suss, Ches, Salop 1740, 8vo, 88pp. (CR.2017/TP1)

**582**  *Thomas Pennant* (1726–1798): Yorks, Notts, Derbys, Staffs, Ches 1773, 8vo, 116pp. (CR.2017/TP2)

**583**  *do*. Suss, Hants, I of W, Dorset, Devon, Corn late 18 c, 8vo, 124pp. (CR.2017/TP11)

**584**  *do*. Yorks, Derbys, Ches, Cheltenham, Wye Valley, Leics c.1792–1800, 4to, 72pp. (CR.2017/TP73)

**585**  *David Pennant senr* (1763–1841): Suff, London, Berks, Warws, Salop, Powys 1805, 4to, (CR.2017/F207)

**586**  *Agnes Carlile*: Warws 1870, 8vo, 38pp. (CR.2119/1)

# West Sussex
West Sussex Record Office, County Hall, Chichester, PO19 1RN

**587**  *Rev G A Langdale* of Compton: Lake District 1834, 4to, 121pp, illus. (Add.MS.19,533)

**588**  *Charles Matthew Buckle*: Scotland 1866, 8vo, c.120pp. (Buckle MS.535)

**589**  *do*. Scotland 1869, 8vo, c.120pp. (Buckle MS.536)

# West Yorkshire
West Yorkshire Archive Service

Bradford District Archives, 15 Canal Road, Bradford, BD1 4AT

**590**  *Irvine Lightowler*: Yorks, Lancs 1923–1981, 18 vols, 4to, 3,411pp. (53D86)

Caldergate District Archives, Calderdale Central Library, Northgate House, Northgate, Halifax, HX1 1UN

**591**  *John Sutcliffe* of Halifax: Halifax to London 1797, 12mo, 70pp. (HAS:681)

**592**  *Anne Lister* of Halifax: Manchester, Liverpool, London, S England 1831, 8vo, 33pp. (SH:7/ML/TR/11)

Kirklees District Archives, Central Library, Princess Alexandra Walk, Huddersfield, HD1 2SU

No relevant diaries

Leeds District Archives, Chapeltown Road, Sheepscar, Leeds, LS7 3AP

**593** *Anon*: Maidstone to Yorkshire 1826, 12mo, 155pp. (Ga/Z 9)

Wakefield Headquarters, Registry of Deeds, Newstead Road, Wakefield, WF1 2DE

**594** *Rev J Hudson* of Dodworth: Harrogate, Buxton, Teignmouth, Cleethorpes, Whitby 1861–1886, 2 vols, 4to. (D25/3/20–21)

Yorkshire Archaeological Society, Claremont, Clarendon Road, Leeds, LS2 9NZ

**595** *Ralph Thoresby of Leeds* (1658–1725): N England, Yorks, London 1677–1724, 5 vols, 4to and 12mo. (MS21–25). Extracts published in J. Hunter, *The Diary of Ralph Thoresby F.R.S., author of the Topography of Leeds*, London, 1830, 2 vols.

**596** *Edward Southwell?*: London, Herts, Cambs, Northants, Bucks, Leics, Yorks 1724, 8vo, 60pp. (MS328). Extracts published in *Country Life*, 1, 8 February 1973.

**597** *L Noble*: Yorks, Cumb, Lancs 1774, 12mo, 32pp. (DD70/142)

**598** *Anon*: Wales, Liverpool, Carlisle early 19 c, 4to, 46pp. (DD56/S)

**599** *Joseph Lindley* (1806–1885): Yorks 1830, 8vo, 48pp. (MD280/18)

**600** *William Best Robinson?*: I of W 1863, 8vo, 48pp., illus. (MS794)

**601** *Leonard Jacques* of Easby Abbey: Lake District, Carlisle, Newcastle upon Tyne, Durham 1863, 4to, 373pp. (MS727/3)

**602** *do.* Yorks, Notts, Lancs 1867–1869, 4to, 13pp. (MS727/5)

## Wiltshire
Wiltshire Record Office, County Hall, Trowbridge, BA14 8JG

**603** *Anon*: Carlisle to Lichfield 1757, 8vo, 25pp. (1742 Box 79)

**604** *Charles, Lord Bruce, and Mr Brand*: N England, Scotland 1789, 8vo, 120pp. (1300/vol xxvi)

**605** *Sir Richard Colt Hoare*: Som 1808, 8vo, 25pp. (383/932)

**606** *Anon*: Wales 1833, 8vo, 22pp. (473/387)

**607** *Charlotte Hobhouse*: Wales 1855, 12mo, 58pp. (112/2/7)

**608** *Miss Grove and Miss W Portman*: Som, Devon, Cornwall, Dorset 1820, 4to, 44pp. (865/572)

# Index of Diarists

Please note that the numbers refer to the entries and not to the page in the catalogue.

# Index of Places

## England

**England** 88, 99, 180, 181, 216, 321, 323, 325, 342, 365, 378, 386–388, 434, 502, 508, 538, 543–545, 550, 556, 564, 591, 603

Cotswolds 307

East Anglia 287, 502, 506, 563

Home Counties 365

Irish Sea 333

Midlands 132, 451, 452, 520

Northern England 132, 210, 360, 379, 380, 470, 519, 520, 546, 577, 595, 604

R Severn 151

South Coast 256, 258–260, 333, 507, 576

South East England 563

Southern England 149, 213, 251, 451

West Country 132, 140, 273, 349, 385, 438, 473, 539, 546, 551–553, 577

West Midlands 341, 345, 349

Wye Valley 22, 50, 151, 223, 281, 283, 291, 370, 374, 459, 584

## English Counties

**Bedfordshire** 15, 25, 30, 44, 156, 179, 189, 491, 493

R Ouse 30

**Berkshire** 3, 6, 8, 24, 25, 31, 40, 56–58, 61, 103, 154, 295, 326, 346, 442, 443, 485, 566, 574, 585

Windsor 148, 395, 397

**Buckinghamshire** 1, 2, 5, 11, 44, 185, 187, 221, 331, 470, 478, 566, 596

**Cambridgeshire** 2, 5–7, 10, 39, 103, 156, 178, 183, 188, 210, 343, 365, 401, 452, 478, 523, 524, 596

Cambridge 24, 440, 493, 515

Peterborough 227, 398

Ely 227

**Channel Islands** 36, 201, 256, 286, 362, 376, 502, 517, 554

**Cheshire** 17, 24, 39–41, 50, 51, 57, 60, 69, 156, 157, 185, 186, 308, 316, 389, 392, 492, 499, 581, 582, 584

Chester 24, 59, 75, 152, 168, 175, 286, 364, 369

**Cornwall** 12, 18, 66, 70, 82, 84, 86, 108, 110, 113, 115, 122, 128, 146, 147, 156, 190, 205, 227, 234,

244, 248, 265, 289, 304, 306, 327, 361, 405, 429, 489, 504, 507, 514, 536, 563, 583, 608

Bude 29

Falmouth 257

Polperro 36

Isles of Scilly 257

**Cumbria** 40, 48, 97, 142, 183, 184, 200, 217, 218, 252, 423, 454, 469, 534, 568, 597

Allonby 95

Carlisle 96, 152, 168, 176, 270, 463, 598, 601, 603

Greystoke 96

Lake District 26, 29, 39, 50, 77–79, 96, 98, 100–102, 105, 118, 121, 122, 125, 132, 156, 160, 167, 176, 182, 191, 196, 199, 200, 205, 218, 219, 224, 230, 235, 238, 242, 246, 280, 288, 301, 322, 335, 348, 250, 359, 370, 381, 383, 403, 411, 456, 457, 465, 507, 510, 512, 513, 518, 559, 563, 565, 587, 601

Penrith 568

Solway Moss 456, 457

Workington 92

**Devon** 12, 18, 23, 33, 38, 58, 69, 70, 83, 88, 103, 108, 110–112, 115, 116, 124, 128, 154, 156, 169, 197,

Printed in the United Kingdom for Her Majesty's Stationery Office
Dd. 240060    1/89    C25